A Fiction Lover's Devotional

21 Days
of
Love

Stories that
Celebrate
Treasured
Relationships

BroadStreet
PUBLISHING

Published by BroadStreet Publishing Group, LLC
Racine, Wisconsin, USA
www.broadstreetpublishing.com

21 Days of Love
Stories that Celebrate Treasured Relationships

ISBN: 978-1-4245-5154-5 (hard cover)
ISBN: 978-1-4245-5155-2 (e-book)

Cover design by Chris Garborg at www.garborgdesign.com
Interior by Katherine Lloyd at www.TheDESKonline.com

Stock or custom editions of BroadStreet Publishing titles may be purchased in bulk for educational, business, ministry, fundraising, or sales promotional use. For information, please e-mail info@broadstreetpublishing.com.

Printed in China

Contents

hat are your favorite Valentine's Day memories? Cherry-flavored lollipops from childhood? Sweethearts candies with love-inspired messages like *Be Mine* and *Let's Kiss* that sent your heart soaring in junior high? The cute red teddy bear holding a heart-shaped pillow trimmed in lace with *I Love You* stitched across the satin, given to you by your first love from high school?

How about as you grew older? Whitman's chocolates? Love-themed dances? Hallmark cards scrawled with forever promises? Does Valentine's Day mark an anniversary of a first dance, first kiss, first date … or the day you said, "I do"?

When we are in love, we look forward to February 14. Sometimes we even dress up for it—in red and pink and maybe a touch of black. We exchange gifts and greeting cards, candies and trinkets on this special day.

Yet for some, Valentine's Day is a reminder that "no one loves me." Painful memories spring to the surface, those that have been kept inside for so long, the anguish they cause feels "normal."

I've been in all of those situations. My memories of grade school are both whimsical and hurtful. The pretty little girl in the desk next to mine received the cute card that said, "Will You Be Mine?" and a heart-shaped lollipop, while I received the generic card with a picture of an owl asking, "Whoooo will be my Valentine?"

Apparently the little girl in the seat next to mine was special and I was ordinary.

I enjoyed some high school Valentine's Day dances. But there were other times when I stood against the wall, wondering why no one wanted to boogie with me. And as a single young woman, I had years when the holiday meant long-stemmed roses and candlelight dinners and others that saw me playing Solitaire until bedtime.

For many, Valentine's Day correlates with wedding anniversaries ... which can be romantic, but also frustrating. Just try getting a dinner reservation for your anniversary on the busiest date night of in the year.

Over the course of my life, I have learned one all-important thing: *I am loved.* Whether there's a "certain someone" to celebrate the day with or not, God loves me. Jesus is my eternal Bridegroom. And even though He doesn't send out sentimental Hallmark cards, He has given an entire book with one central theme: His love for me (and for you too). He has also given me dear family members and friends. Treasured relationships.

As you read these stories, think of the people who have poured love into your life. Think too about the treasure of the ultimate love, the love of God and of His Son, Jesus.

Eva Marie Everson is the multiple-award-winning author of both fiction and nonfiction works, including *Reflections of God's Holy Land* and *Waiting for Sunrise*. She is president of Word Weavers International, director of the Florida Christian Writers Conference, vice president of BelieversTrust, and acquisitions editor of Firefly Southern Fiction. Eva Marie is a wife, mother, and grandmother. She and her husband make their home along Lake Kathryn in Florida, where they are owned by their dog, Poods.

1

Ballerina Girl

by Lori Freeland

Savannah's Sunday evening prayer vigil had been a bust. God didn't love her. If He did, He wouldn't have taken everything away. And He wouldn't have let today come and drag her back to Brighton High's dim and depressing hallways.

Returning to school was a cruel joke. Who cared if she finished senior year? Dance was out. Julliard was out. Her future was out. All crushed in a single stupid moment.

Savannah slumped in the back of senior English Lit, but her wilted pose didn't stop the rubbernecking or mute the whispers. Her first day back, after two months of being MIA, was awkwardly agonizing. Tomorrow she'd wrap herself in her black hoodie with the earbuds. Or get the flu until graduation.

Logan entered just as the bell rang, bypassing his regular seat to claim the empty spot beside her. His swoon-worthy smile hit her like a triple espresso. She'd been addicted to that smile since seventh grade.

He ran a hand through his sleep-styled hair. "Morning, Swan Lake." His voice was still early-morning deep.

"Don't call me that." She was done with dance. Now she needed to be done with her covert crush. Unfortunately, the we-love-Logan butterflies swirling in her stomach didn't agree. Why couldn't Logan be arrogant? Or mean? Or ugly?

"So …" His blue eyes pinned her in place. "I came by your house … right after … you know." He didn't seem to notice the dark circles living underneath her eyes. He didn't act like anything about her had changed. He just grinned like he'd looked forward to her return as much as she'd dreaded it. "Why wouldn't you see me?"

She shifted in her chair. "A lot of people came by." At first.

"Doesn't matter." Her nonanswer rolled off him in typical Logan fashion. "You're back now."

"Not by choice." After Matt ditched her, everyone else did too. She'd become social Siberia. So why did Logan sit next to her?

He leaned close, so close all she could smell was his woodsy shower gel, and those clueless belly butterflies threw him a pep rally. For two wonderful seconds he made her feel almost normal. Almost like the old Savannah.

Then Matt swaggered through the door. His gaze hit on every girl—except her—before he picked the redhead on the drill team. He sat beside her and ran a finger down her bare arm. All player. Zero class.

"Jealous looks bad on your ex." Logan scooted his chair so his shoulder brushed hers.

"Yeah. Because *that's* what jealousy looks like." There was no way she could compete with the redhead. Not anymore. "Pretty sure Matt knows what he gave up."

"Pretty sure he doesn't." Logan nudged her shoulder. "Let's go to the Valentine's dance."

"You're hilarious." If he were anyone else, she'd shield herself for the punch line. But Logan had never been cruel. And he didn't seem to care that she'd come back to school … different.

Up front, Mrs. Gates started class, leaving no more time to talk.

When the lecture ended, Logan leaned over and whispered, "Can't wait for Friday night." And then he left. As if his cut-and-run could somehow cancel out the Mount-Everest reason she'd have to say no.

By Tuesday, Savannah convinced herself Logan had a momentary break with reality when he asked her to the dance. But during anatomy lab, he dropped onto Matt's abandoned stool wearing an even bigger grin than yesterday. "I poached my brother's black suit and red tie. You'd look hot in red."

She wouldn't look hot in anything. "Not going."

He grabbed a dissection tray and stared at the poor baby shark up next for mutilation. "I'll pick you up Friday at eight."

Hoping he wouldn't see the almost-tears in her eyes, she handed him a pair of gloves. "I'll be in bed at eight."

"You're seventeen." He laughed. "Not seventy."

Was there a difference anymore?

She reached for a scalpel, but he grabbed it first. "I'll butcher. You scribe." He dangled a spiral notebook in front of her.

Writing up the lab report used to be Matt's job. She glanced at her ex, who was busy working conquest number two—a brunette from JV Cheer.

Holding the scalpel like a dart, Logan aimed it at Matt. "You're bailing on life because of *him*?"

"You *know* why I'm bailing."

Logan put down the knife and rested his gloved fingers on her arm. "You don't have to give up everything, you know."

"Drop it." The warmth of his touch heated her face. She looked away.

"Dropped." He squeezed her hand. "But just for today." He picked up the scalpel and positioned it to make the first cut.

Wednesday, Logan swung by art club, the only creative outlet Savannah hadn't yet quit. "I was thinking dinner before the dance."

"Seriously." Her brush fell into her lap and red paint spattered her favorite jeans. "Why are you doing this?"

"Team Savannah had a vacancy." He pulled up a chair and straddled it. "I want the spot."

"You want to date me?" Her voice mirrored her disbelief. "Now?" She glanced at her paint-spattered lap. He felt sorry for her. That had to be it.

He shrugged. "You've always been with Matt. I don't date other guys' girls."

"You don't date at all." She grabbed a paper towel and dabbed at the wet paint.

"You weren't available."

"I don't want your pity date."

"That's too bad." He hopped off the stool and leaned down to look into her eyes. "I'd take your pity date any day."

Thursday, Savannah sat in the lunchroom alone, not eating the burrito special.

Logan sat across from her. "Why aren't you over there?" He motioned to the drill team girls, who'd been stealing glances since she entered the cafeteria.

The last routine they'd done together played through her head in 3D, making her legs ache for release. Watching her ex-friends, her *dance* friends, killed something inside her. She'd give anything to be *over there*. But Logan didn't get it. "They don't want me." Matt didn't want her. Why would anyone else? She was useless now. "They're busy. And …"

"And what?"

The sincerity in his eyes made her crave things she'd never have. "And I don't dance anymore."

"We'll see." He brushed his fingers over her cheek and then pulled his disappearing act again.

Friday night, Savannah still felt the warmth of Logan's touch on her face. Every time she pictured that moment, those traitorous butterflies did the one thing she couldn't—a perfect pirouette.

At seven o'clock, she got comfy on the family room sectional, threw a blanket over her pink flannel pajamas, and turned on a movie. Whatever had been going on between her and Logan this week was over. If she cared about him, she wouldn't saddle him with her impossible issues. Issues that wouldn't end at graduation.

At eight on the dot, she heard the doorbell. Before she could protest, her mom led Logan into the room and left.

Dressed in a black suit, gray shirt, and red tie, he looked good. Way too good for someone like her.

"I hadn't pictured you in pink *flannel*." He ran his gaze over her. "But I can make it work." With a goofy grin, he touched his belt buckle. "Boxers with hearts okay with you?"

"I think my mom would say no." A small laugh came out of her throat, even though she wanted to cry. "Why are you here?" She shook her head. "You should go to the dance with someone who deserves you."

"Why do you push everyone away?" He took a few steps toward her.

"I don't."

"Yeah, you do. You act like you're damaged goods."

"I am!" She flipped off the blanket and pointed to her legs. The legs that used to bend and stretch and plié. The legs that got her into Julliard. The legs that no longer worked.

Logan sat on the wheelchair next to the ottoman. Like the chair meant nothing.

"I lost everything. My boyfriend. My future. Myself." She pressed her fingers to her eyes. "All because I let Matt drive when I knew he'd been drinking."

"You got in the car to stop him." Logan's voice was soft. "You—"

"I screwed up! Matt's fine and I'm … never going to be fine again." She slapped her stupid, useless legs.

Logan got off the wheelchair and sat on the ottoman facing her. He took her hands. "Your legs aren't who you are." He pulled her against his chest and held her close. "And I really like who you are."

His arms were warm, safe, strong. She cried out the hurt and anger and frustration she'd buried since that night. She wept until his shirt stuck to her cheek.

"I ruined your shirt." She sniffed against his damp chest.

"Nah. You made my night." He framed her face with his palms and looked into her eyes. "I got to save a damsel in distress. Top of my bucket list all along." He gave her his special Logan smile.

This time when the butterflies swooned, she encouraged them. "Saving Savannah was on your bucket list, huh?" She wiped her eyes with the heel of her hand.

"Yep." Logan pressed his lips against her forehead. "Along with something else." He brushed his thumbs down her cheek, leaned in, and kissed her. "Two thousand eighteen," he whispered. "That's the number of days I've wanted to do that. Since seventh grade." He hugged her tight.

"Maybe we *should* go to the dance." And maybe God loved her after all. He'd sent her Logan. And Logan made her feel as if she could do anything.

Life Application

Sometimes bad things happen and we don't understand why. It wasn't Savannah's choice to break up with Matt or to stop dancing. But God wanted to do something new in her life.

God wants what's best for us. He sees our future and He knows how to direct our paths. It's easy to trust Him when those paths match up with what we want. It's harder to trust when they don't. That's where faith steps in. That's when trust is built.

God tells us, "Forget the former things; do not dwell on the past. See, I am doing a new thing! Now it springs up; do you not perceive it? I am making a way in the wilderness and streams in the wasteland" (Isaiah 43:18–19).

Does God want to do something new in your life? Will you let Him?

About the Author

Lori Freeland is a writing teacher and coach for the North Texas Christian Writers and a contributor to Crosswalk.com and Believe.com. She's addicted to flavored coffee and imaginary people. When she's not writing inspirational articles, she's working on several young-adult novels. Visit her website, www .lafreeland.com, or look for L. A. Freeland on Facebook.

2

A Valentine for Teacher

by Renae Brumbaugh

February 13, 1908

"Hurry, Miss Wilson. He might be there already!"

"You go on ahead, Alexander. I'll be along directly."

"You sure, ma'am? Ma said to escort you home ever' day, and we ain't home yet."

"We're *not* home yet."

"That's what I said."

"No, you said … Never mind. We can see your house from here. I'm sure, under the circumstances, your mother won't mind you running ahead. I'll explain to her that I told you to do so."

"Thanks, Miss Wilson. You're swell!" Ten-year-old Alex Thompson called that last part of the sentence over his shoulder.

Kate watched her student practically grow wings and soar

the rest of the way to his house, where some beloved cousin was scheduled to arrive. It was all the boy had spoken of for the last three weeks. And considering her room in the Thompson home was the only spare bedroom, she'd wondered if she'd be expected to move her things to the barn during the visit.

But no one had asked, and she hadn't offered. After all, the school board was paying for her room and board at the Thompsons' home. It was *her room*, at least for the next three months. *Probably the rest of my life, the way things look.*

Kate loved teaching school. She loved the smell of the books, the grit of chalk dust on her hands, the clang-clang of the big brass bell. She even loved the wet-puppy stench of her charges after coming in from recess.

What she *didn't* love were the strict rules enforced by the local school board. Oh, they were the same as practically every other district. Early curfew. No loitering in town. No dilly-dallying at ice cream parlors. And absolutely no men.

Much as she loved her job, she didn't want to be an old-maid schoolmarm forever. She would either have to refuse a contract for the following school year and take a job at a mercantile or dress shop, or resign herself to another year of no male prospects whatsoever.

Even if she did find other employment, there were no guarantees that Prince Charming would magically appear. And none of her other employment options would allow her the delight of books and learning, the thrill of discovery, every single day.

And it wasn't like she could go home. After Papa died two springs ago and Mama moved in with Charlie and Beth and their six children . . . well, Kate knew her older brother would find space for her. But she didn't want to be a burden.

So she taught. And prayed, every day, about whether or not she was really called to remain unmarried for the rest of her life, just so she could teach school.

She sure hoped not. Once again, she breathed the prayer she'd uttered every day for the last few months. "God, You know my heart. Show me what to do."

At least a pleasant task lay in store this evening. In anticipation of the Thompsons' guest, Kate had purchased bits of bright fabric, scraps of lace, and some old buttons from Mrs. Taylor. The seamstress was happy to sell her a whole box of odds and ends for a penny. Since Valentine's Day was tomorrow, Kate would go straight to her room to make cards for her twelve students. That would give the Thompson family time with their cousin.

The wide wooden porch stairs creaked with each step. The mild February sun warmed her shoulders, and Kate considered resting a moment in one of the painted rocking chairs. She turned to take in the peaceful landscape of the Texas Piney Woods.

"You must be Miss Wilson."

The voice was deep and sultry, like an August day had invaded the February landscape. Kate pulled her gaze from the pine trees to an even more brilliant sight.

Standing before her was the most handsome man she'd seen in all her days. Six foot four, at least, from the way he bent his head beneath the doorframe. Wide shoulders that rivaled Paul Bunyan's, she was sure. Blond curls framed a sun-bronzed face and white teeth. An easy grin split across his features, forcing a pair of dimples to wink at her.

She never knew dimples could go that deep.

His friendly, wide-set eyes were a color she couldn't quite describe. Caramel, perhaps? With a hint of moss-green toward the centers. Tiny lines crinkled on either side of those eyes like shooting stars.

She stood there, mouth hanging open, peering out from beneath her hooded cloak like a stunned chicken. When he stepped aside to let her pass, she attempted to gather her spilled wits. It felt a bit like trying to spoon an egg back into its shell.

His brawn filled the space, and her shoulder brushed his arm as she entered the Thompson home.

"There you are!" Esther Thompson came rushing to the doorway, Alexander in her wake. "I was a little worried when Alex came home without ya."

"Oh, I encouraged him to run ahead. It's such a beautiful day, and I was enjoying the sunshine."

The woman scowled at her son. "You're forgiven this time. But don't let it happen again. Miss Wilson's a lady, and a gentleman always escorts a lady to her destination."

"Yes'm." The boy looked duly chastised.

"Miss Wilson, this here's my nephew Will. He's stoppin' through on his way to Houston. He's got some business down there."

The man extended his hand, and she took it. "Will Parker. It's an honor to meet you, Miss Wilson." The words rolled off his tongue with an odd combination of education and country-boy twang.

"Pleased to meet you, Mr. Parker." She withdrew her hand, but the warmth of his fingers on her gloved palm remained. Their eyes held for a moment longer than necessary, and Kate wondered if her face was as red as it was hot.

She thought about the science experiment she'd led in class a couple of weeks ago using oversized magnets. There was definitely an invisible pull in her spirit that wanted to center itself on this man. Which was ridiculous. She knew nothing about him. He could be the leader in a three-ring traveling circus for all she knew.

"Can I help with dinner, Mrs. Thompson?" she asked.

"Nonsense. You've worked hard all day. Here, let me take your things; I'll put them on your bed for you. Why don't you keep Will company while I pop the rolls into the oven." A tiny smirk lit the woman's face. Then she gave Kate a quick, sly wink. Was she matchmaking?

Oh, dear. If the school board found out about this, she could lose her job.

Esther Thompson didn't seem the type to set a trap. Why, she was one of the most genuine, caring women Kate had ever had the privilege to know.

With no time to contemplate hidden intentions, she sat in the cushioned chair beside the fireplace. Will Parker took the seat across from her. Her tongue felt swollen and sticky.

"Alex has mentioned you in his letters to me," Will said. "You've made quite an impression on him."

"He's a fine young man with a keen mind. I enjoy teaching him."

"He is certainly a sharp boy. I've thought of grooming him to assist in my business one day, when he's old enough."

"What kind of business are you in?"

"Will's in oil," Alex nearly shouted. "He took me to one of the well sites last summer, and I got to see a gusher."

"Oil. How fascinating. And extremely profitable."

"The business kind of found me, actually. Some men showed up at my daddy's cotton farm six years ago and offered to pay him to let them dig for oil in one of his fallow fields. He figured he had nothing to lose. Next thing we know, there's black liquid spraying all over the cotton."

"Oh, dear. That doesn't sound good for the crop."

"It wasn't. But it all worked out in the end."

Mr. Thompson entered through the back door, and Mrs. Thompson called them all to the table. After a prayer, the conversation flowed as thick and delicious as brown gravy on roast beef. More than once, Kate felt Will's eyes on her, and she tried to keep her hands steady. The last thing she needed was to drip butter on her blouse.

When the table had been cleared, Kate remembered her valentines. As much as she hated to end this, she needed to get those done. "It's been delightful, but I must excuse myself and prepare for tomorrow."

"Aw, whatcha gotta do that's so important it can't wait?"

"If you must know, Alexander, I'm working on a surprise for all my students."

"For Valentine's Day?" Will gave her a knowing smile.

"Why, yes."

"Oh, let us help you. Alex can keep a secret, can't you, Son?" Esther Thompson sent her boy one of those "Mama's watching you so you'd better be good" looks.

"Yes, ma'am."

"It's settled then. Just bring your supplies into the parlor." The woman gave Kate another smirk. How embarrassing.

And fun.

For the next hour and a half, Kate sat with the Thompson family, stitching and stuffing bits of cotton into tiny heart-shaped pillows. Even Will and Mr. Thompson helped, though Will's enormous hands were clumsy with the task. He finished one pillow in the time it took Kate to do four. At last, she attached little scraps of colored paper to each, with the words "Happy Valentine's Day from Miss Wilson" written on them.

When the task was done, she stood. "Thank you all so much. The job went a lot faster with your help. But I really must retire now."

They all said their good nights. Shortly after Kate crawled under her sheets, she heard the front door open and close, and footsteps go out toward the barn. Will must be staying there.

It was a long time before she went to sleep that night.

The next morning, Will was not at the breakfast table. Kate tried not to show her disappointment. How silly of her to think she was anything more than the old-maid schoolteacher to a man like Will Parker.

As she tied her cloak around her, Esther handed her the box of valentines.

"Thank you."

"There's a note on the bottom for you. From Will."

Kate sucked in her breath, and her heart used the inside of her chest as a punching bag.

"You can read it now if you want." Esther walked back toward the kitchen. Bless her soul!

Kate set the box on the table and found the note.

Dear Miss Wilson,

I enjoyed spending time with you last evening. Your students are blessed to have you as their teacher.

I'll be back in about a week. After that, I'd be most honored if you would permit me to write to you.

Happy Valentine's Day.

Will Parker

Life Application

"Delight yourself in the LORD, and He will give you the desires of your heart" (Psalm 37:4 ESV).

Most of us understand the concept of delighting in God. As Christians, we're supposed to center our thoughts on Him, serve Him, and please Him. But we often forget that He delights in us! God loves us. He created us, and He formed the desires in our hearts. He longs to thrill us with breath-catching fulfillment of our innermost dreams.

But first, we need to trust Him. Instead of scheming and manipulating to make things happen the way we think they should, He wants us to ask Him for wisdom. When we let go, joyfully serve God, and trust Him with the future, He often turns our dreams into reality in unexpected ways.

About the Author

Renae Brumbaugh has authored nearly twenty books and has landed on the ECPA Bestseller List twice. She's sold hundreds of articles to national publications and has won awards for her humor. She's married to her own handsome country boy, and they have four nearly perfect children, two not-so-perfect dogs, and a dozen chickens. Learn more at RenaeBrumbaugh.com.

3

Secondhand Life

by Cindy Woodsmall

*J*emma pulled another pan of biscuits out of the oven. She could hear her husband's muted voice as he stood on the driveway talking to … *her*. Did he think his wife didn't know how he felt? Jemma pushed the hurt aside. He was simply infatuated with Fannie Ruth. His feelings would evaporate if given time.

Or would they grow stronger?

She pulled her focus back to the six energetic children squirming in their kitchen chairs while they ate breakfast and jabbered. Rays of sunlight had chased away darkness only minutes ago, and an early-morning summer breeze drifted through the windows. A milk cow mooed softly from the pasture. These were the things she would hold on to, the good parts. Of late, she was more grateful than ever for the hard work on an Amish dairy farm.

"Mamm?" Five-year-old Lydiann smiled, holding up the crust of her toast, showing Jemma she'd eaten all but a few bites.

"*Gut* job." Jemma winked at her.

The four younger children's smiling faces were smeared with jelly or butter or yogurt. Elam and Ben were teens now. They towered over her when standing, but just yesterday they'd been more than a foot shorter than she. Well, actually that was five years ago. That's when she'd joined this big, beautiful family as a nanny … of sorts.

Arlan's wife had died giving birth in this home, and he had to bury the love of his life. His mother moved in with him to help raise the children, but with grief weighing on them and six children ranging from newborn to twelve years old, Arlan and his Mamm needed help. When Jemma heard of Arlan's plight, she was living in a different state. Her dry-goods store had closed due to the downturn in the economy, and she needed a job. More than that, she needed something to keep her mind occupied so she didn't feel like a failure.

Right now she felt like the biggest failure the Amish community had ever known.

Heartache threatened to break free. She squelched it. At least the children loved her. She hadn't realized when she came here at thirty-nine years old that love was every bit as tangible to the heart as food was to an empty belly.

Fannie Ruth's laughter floated through the open windows. *Don't look, Jemma. Just stay away from the window.*

Against her inner warning, she leaned over the sink and peered outside. Arlan stood with his arms folded, nodding at Fannie Ruth's comments. Although his straw hat cast a shadow over his face, it didn't hide his grin.

Two years after Jemma began working here, Arlan had, for all intents and purposes, been forced to marry her. Arlan's sister, who lived two hours away, had given birth to her second set of twins in less than three years, and his Mamm had to move in with her. Jemma couldn't remain living in the same house as Arlan unless they married.

Since the day of their wedding, she'd known the relationship could end this way. Still, until a few weeks ago, she'd thought her husband had come to love her too. It had been a slow process, to be sure, one filled with grief and compromise as the two banded together for the sake of the children. For four months after marrying, they hadn't even shared a bedroom.

Fannie Ruth, a single woman fifteen years younger than Jemma, came by each morning to sell eggs. At first, she came into the house and talked while making the delivery, which grated on Jemma's nerves. But ever since Arlan began building an addition to their home five weeks ago, he made sure he was outside, ready to engage in a private conversation with her. And each day she stayed longer than the day before.

Jemma sat at the kitchen table and intertwined her fingers, trying to keep her hands from trembling. Years of sacrifice and bonding—for what? For her husband to take every opportunity he could find to talk to Fannie Ruth.

Don't think about it.

Jemma focused on each child, counting her blessings. They couldn't feel more hers if she'd given birth to them.

Fannie Ruth's laughter burst into the room, penetrating Jemma's will.

Enough!

She rushed outside.

From the corner of his eye, Arlan saw a blur of a sage-green cape dress bursting out the front door. His wife stopped short, looking at him directly for the first time in weeks, her eyes filled with bewilderment.

The tool belt around his waist became heavier, and the silence of the construction site needled him.

"Good morning, Jemma." Fannie Ruth shifted, looking uncomfortable. "Lovely day. And you are a blessed woman to—"

"*Ya*, I am." Jemma took the basket of eggs from Fannie Ruth. "*Denki.*" She nodded once, without a hint of her usual gentleness. "I can't imagine how you get all the deliveries made in a day."

Fannie Ruth's eyes widened, and she glanced at Arlan. "You're right. I need to be on my way." She climbed into her carriage and waved good-bye.

Arlan raised his hand to offer a friendly gesture of farewell. After Fannie Ruth's carriage pulled out of the driveway, Jemma flung the basket of eggs at his feet and stormed off. The screen door slammed shut behind her. Arlan stared at the gooey mess on the gravel driveway.

Jemma wasn't one to overreact to anything, and her anger confounded him as much as some of her other behavior of late. Their relationship situation was unusual, but it worked beyond anything he'd hoped or prayed for. Or at least it usually did.

But lately, the air smoldered with Jemma's displeasure. He missed their morning chats over coffee before the children got up. Missed her holding his hand during prayers before and after supper. Missed the way she smiled at him from across the room. Missed going to sleep holding her or waking wrapped in her arms.

He removed his tool belt. Work could wait. He headed for the house.

When Jemma first arrived five years ago, Arlan had been too grief-stricken to speak. Jemma had helped his Mamm for at least a month, maybe two or three, before he even realized she was a real person. Until then she seemed like the rest of his life—a stick figure that dutifully moved about with no sense of connection to anything normal. He didn't know how long he remained in that stupor, but little by little she called to him to join life again—to take joy in his children, to appreciate the way sunlight danced across the yard and played with the shadows of trees, to once again taste the food he put in his mouth.

Eventually he saw someone with two kind eyes and a pair of gentle hands that worked night and day to make sure his baby thrived and to help his children navigate through the trauma. It was probably a year before he came to himself enough to realize she had thoughts and emotions that needed and deserved his respect. It was her nature to give a lot and ask for little.

Whatever was going on of late wasn't normal.

He walked inside. Jemma stood at the kitchen sink, washing dishes. The children were clearing items off the table and taking glasses and plates to her. As usual, the room was filled with conversations and busyness.

"Elam," Arlan called to his seventeen-year-old son. "You and Ben hitch a wagon to Ol' Bo and take everyone for a ride. Jemma and I need to talk."

Despite the questions in his son's eyes, Elam nodded. "You heard Dad. Put everything down right now and let's go." Elam snapped his fingers. "Move quick and I'll buy you a soft drink at the gas station."

Dishes and flatware clinked and clattered as the children emptied their hands on the nearest cabinet.

Arlan pulled cash from his billfold and passed it to Elam. It was good thinking to offer everyone something as prized as a soft drink. The children's footfalls hit fast and heavy while they hurried out the door, laughing and calling dibs of who would sit where in the back of the wagon. Soon the walls stopped echoing and silence reigned.

He grabbed a kitchen towel and removed a plate from the dish rack.

In those first two years, with four children under six years old, how many nights had they washed dishes together, talking quietly long after everyone was asleep? Other evenings they would iron and fold clothes—all the while getting to know each other and learning to draw strength from each other.

Jemma had accepted that he had come undone when his wife died, and she helped him find the pieces. He'd learned to love her in a way he'd never loved before. And the friendship they developed was unlike any he'd ever known. But he'd had little to offer Jemma except long days of hard work as she raised someone else's children.

"I … I miss you, Jem." He set the plate in the cabinet and grabbed another one to dry. "I don't know this new woman who's removed herself from our bedroom to sleep on the couch, rarely talks to me, and pitched a basket of eggs at my feet." He set another dried plate in the cabinet. "But I want to know her."

She stared at the murky dishwater, tears welling in her eyes.

"Jemma." He placed his hands on her shoulders and turned her toward him. He dried her dripping hands with the towel. "I love you." He lifted her chin. "You know that, right?"

She closed her eyes, tears falling as she shook her head. "You needed me, and now you're stuck with me."

His heart sank. If that's what she thought, he had failed her. If he'd traveled throughout Amish country, trying to find a good mother for his children and an excellent wife for himself, he could not have matched the woman God brought to him.

"It's true. I did need you. Desperately." He led her to a kitchen chair. She sat, and he crouched beside her. "But as you met all those needs, I saw you for you who are, and I fell in love with you." He caressed her fingers. "I'm not great at explaining my feelings, but you know that." He kissed her hand. "Why are you doubting?"

She shrugged.

"Come on. You threw eggs at my feet." He winked. "Now throw some words my way."

Her pursed lips opened, and he knew she was trying to voice her thoughts. Finally, she whispered, "Lydiann starts school next month."

Ah, the dreaded day when the youngest one entered school. He should've realized that would be tough. "The children won't always have childhood needs. But they will always need you—just as I will, every day for the rest of my life."

Jemma didn't look the least bit convinced. "And what about Fannie Ruth?"

Was that what this was about? "Because of the addition we're building, you've had extra work added to your day, feeding a team of men lunch every day. I've been trying to keep your morning manageable. That's all."

"She could've given you more children." Jemma had been forty-one when they married, so they knew she may not conceive.

"Do I look like I need more children?" He chuckled, then pulled a chair close to hers and sat in it. "I wanted to give you one of your own. I prayed for that, for your sake. But when a man loses a wife to childbirth, he considers it a blessing from God not to have that worry bearing down on him."

She angled her head. "I didn't know that's how you felt."

"There seems to be a good bit of that going around—on both sides."

She swallowed. "It's hard being a secondhand wife."

"What?" He couldn't believe she thought that.

"You were so reluctant for us to marry."

"Oh, Jem, that's not true."

"It is! How many men do you know who sleep on the couch for four months after getting married?"

His heart pounded as her sense of rejection washed over him. Why hadn't he talked to her about this before?

"Okay." He removed his straw hat and tossed it onto the table. "In my effort to protect your feelings, I have clearly kept too much to myself." He caressed her cheek. "I loved you, Jemma, or I wouldn't have asked you to marry me. But we needed time. I slept on the couch because I didn't want to chance memories of my first wife entering my mind during our first time together."

Understanding shone in her eyes. As the moments passed, the revelation deepened. "You were safeguarding our relationship?"

"I was trying to."

"And it worked?"

He nodded. By the time they finally consummated their vows, he could think of nothing but her and the life God had blessed them with.

"So I … I'm not a secondhand wife?"

"Not at all." He guided her lips to his. Then he rested his forehead on hers. "What we have is special and unique. It's us—wounds, blemishes, strength, and great beauty, all rolled into one."

Life Application

We are all fragile in one way or another. And despite how much effort we may put into a situation, we often get our feelings hurt.

Sometimes I'm so busy trying to keep up with work and the needs of my family members that I'm surprised when they remind me that I am loved. Many of us are so busy trying to do good things for God that we forget how much He loves us.

Ephesians 3:16–19 says, "I pray that out of his glorious riches he may strengthen you with power through his Spirit in your inner being, so that Christ may dwell in your hearts through faith. And I pray that you, being rooted and established in love, may have power, together with all the Lord's holy people, to grasp how wide and long and high and deep is the love of Christ, and to know this love that surpasses knowledge—that you may be filled to the measure of all the fullness of God."

About the Author

Cindy Woodsmall is a *New York Times* and CBA best-selling author who has written seventeen works of fiction. Her connection with the Amish community has been widely featured in national media outlets. In 2013, the *Wall Street Journal* listed Cindy as one of the top three most popular authors of Amish fiction. Cindy and her husband reside near the foothills of the North Georgia mountains.

4

More than Dates and Flowers

by Jeanette Hanscome

Kim maneuvered her shopping cart around a display of floral arrangements and checked her list. Valentines for school (princesses for Maddy, soccer for Kaysi). Gifts for the girls. Cupcake cups with hearts on them.

Her soul drooped as she pushed her cart toward the dreaded red and pink aisle.

I hate Valentine's Day.

It was the same routine every year. Pretend it wasn't a big deal to her because "Jesus is the love of my life now." Fight a rush of memories of romantic dinners and bouquets of her favorite flowers. Get weepy as soon as she spotted the first post on Facebook saying, "Date night with my honey. Can't wait!" And process her grief by doing something weird.

The first year after Craig left, she picked up a heart-shaped pizza from Take 'N' Bake for the girls, then took a friend's advice and bought herself a box of chocolates. It felt nice to treat herself, but that didn't erase the longing for romance. It felt … incomplete.

The second year, she decided the world needed a reminder that Valentine's Day was just another money grab for card companies and florists. She posted the true story of Saint Valentine on Facebook and read it to the girls as a bedtime story. She didn't even have the sensitivity to tone down his execution to an age-appropriate level. Maddy had nightmares. Kim's friend Judy invited her out to lunch to see if she was okay and expressed concerned that she seemed to be getting a bit "dark."

Last year Kim watched a romantic movie and ended the evening by signing up for an online matchmaking service. A string of uncomfortable dates made a life of singleness look very attractive.

This year she'd decided it was best to leave Valentine's Day to those who were in love or in elementary school. Let them enjoy it. They had every right. She would not be that friend who sucked the fun out of a joyful occasion just because she didn't have someone to celebrate with.

But as she stared at the heart-covered shelves, she wanted to wail like a two-year-old. *It's not fair. I want to go on a date! Everyone I know will be getting candy and flowers. And I'll hear all about it on social media.*

She took a deep breath, willed her lip to stop trembling, and grabbed two boxes of conversation hearts, her favorite candy as a kid, for Maddy and Kaysi to enjoy.

God, it's been over three years. When am I gonna grow up and get over this?

I love you, she heard Him say.

I know. Was it wrong to wish God sent flowers?

You can still enjoy the day.

How?

The girls would be with their dad. She didn't even have an excuse to buy a heart-shaped pizza.

She found the princess cards, the soccer cards, and a stuffed bear for each of the girls. In her rush to escape the roses, Kim collided with a shopping cart coming around the corner.

"Sorry," she muttered. Then she saw whose cart she'd hit. Teresa, one of the college girls from church she often called on to babysit, stood there, her eyes puffy, her face pale and sleep-deprived. "Hey, Teresa. You okay?"

She smiled. "Yeah. I'm just picking up some cards for the kids at the rec center where I work."

"You look like you're having a rough day."

She blinked away what looked like tears. "My boyfriend and I broke up last night."

Kim searched for some words of sympathy, but only a lame "I'm sorry" popped out.

"Thanks." Teresa sighed. She picked up a stuffed heart with polka-dot arms and legs, then set it back on the shelf. "We were supposed to go to the city for Valentine's Day and have a nice dinner. I guess that's off."

Kim stood there, torn between saying something less than kind about Teresa's boyfriend and suggesting she plan a fun girls' night instead. She'd experienced enough breakups in her life to know that neither would be helpful. She stroked the young woman's arm. "How disappointing."

Teresa ran her hands through her long blonde hair and gazed at the selection in front of her. "I used to like Valentine's Day." She grabbed a box of Puppies & Kittens cards.

"I know what you mean." Kim gave Teresa a hug, wished her a better day, and watched her walk away.

For the rest of the afternoon, and as she headed home from work the next day, and as she squeezed in a few chores before picking up the girls from after-school daycare, Kim felt a deep need to make Valentine's Day a little less painful for Teresa. But how?

She remembered the year she bought herself chocolates and how incomplete it felt.

Kim checked her flip calendar. The verse for the week jumped out at her. "A generous person will prosper; whoever refreshes others will be refreshed" (Proverbs 11:25).

Kim sat beside a laundry basket filled with towels and started folding them. *I'd love to refresh Teresa. But I can't afford a nice dinner in the city.*

She pulled out a hand towel with fading roses along the bottom edge. The flowers were the same shade of pink as the design on a teacup she'd received over a dozen years ago. She and Craig were engaged at the time but had gotten into a fight and broke up. She'd been too depressed to think about what day it was until she went to Bible study and overheard friends chattering about dinner plans and flowers. Before she could get a grip on her emotions, tears filled her eyes.

A woman named Barb wrapped her arm around her. That touch melted Kim's resolve and tears started to drip.

Barb ushered her to the ladies' room so she could fall apart without an audience. She held her and told her how loved she was. "No lack of a boyfriend can change that, honey," she said. Then she invited her to her house for tea and cake. And friendly conversation.

When Barb poured chamomile tea into a delicate rose-printed china cup and set it in front of Kim, she felt special.

Before Kim left, Barb washed and wrapped the teacup, put it in a gift bag, and handed it to her. "Happy Valentine's Day. Keep it as a reminder that you're loved—by God and many others, including me."

That cup had survived moves, two active kids, and several furniture rearrangements. How had Kim forgotten its message? Barb had done a lot more that day than serve her tea and cake and send her home with a present. She'd shown her that she was valuable and loved.

God, how did I become so whiny and self-focused? Why can't I be more like Barb?

"Whoever refreshes others will be refreshed."

Kim checked her watch. If she hurried, she could make it to the store before she picked up the girls.

In the same aisle that she'd sulked through the day before, she reached for a pretty box of chocolates—the good kind, not the type with rubbery centers and waxy coating. Next she found a greeting card showing Snoopy juggling hearts. Teresa liked Snoopy.

Kim headed to the jewelry section and found a simple heart bracelet. Then she whipped out her phone and texted Teresa. *Have you made plans for Valentine's Day?*

No.

Want to come over for dessert and a movie that would make your ex-boyfriend gag?

Really? I would luv to!

Perfect. See you around 7.

On Valentine's evening, Kim set heart-shaped cupcakes and a bowl of popcorn in the center of the coffee table and got out her pretty plates. As soon as Teresa arrived, Kim handed her a gift bag and card. "Happy Valentine's Day."

Teresa's eyes glistened. "For me? Thank you!" She wrapped her arms around Kim. "I was really dreading this day until I got your text."

Kim wanted to assure Teresa that she had many happy Valentine's Days ahead of her, but she knew better than to make such a promise. All she could do was pray that Teresa would come to understand what she clearly needed to grasp herself—that love wasn't about dates and flowers. True joy came with showing love, whether you expected to receive anything or not.

Life Application

When we've been burned by love, occasions like Valentine's Day serve as cruel reminders of what we've lost, or perhaps never had. Once we've worn out our attempts at pretending we don't care about all those silly romantic sentiments, we're left with pain and loneliness.

Doing something nice for yourself can help, but this often leaves us feeling like something is missing. It can be even more fun to show love to someone else.

The act of showing kindness to a friend, or even a stranger, fills us with joy that far surpasses romantic gestures. When we shift our focus from what we wish we had to what might uplift someone else, God opens doors that can give love a whole new meaning.

About the Author

Jeanette Hanscome is the author of five books including *Running with Roselle* (coauthored with blind 9/11 survivor Michael Hingson). Her devotional *Suddenly Single Mom: 52 Messages of Hope, Grace, and Promise* will be published by Worthy Inspired in March 2016. Jeanette lives in the Bay Area where she sings at her church and enjoys being the mom of two amazing sons.

5

Outspoken Love

by Janet Sketchley

ntering the seniors' residence felt like stepping through an airlock in a science fiction movie. Trina scanned the foyer, with its apple-green rocking chairs and brass planters filled with orange and yellow marigolds. Late-afternoon sun shone through the doors behind her, elongating her shadow across the earth-toned tiles. She wrinkled her nose at the taint of antiseptic.

A young woman with gold hoop earrings smiled from the reception desk. "Can I help you find someone?" In the world outside, her lipstick would have been brighter, her voice louder.

Trina hitched her purse strap higher on her shoulder. "I'm here to see Olivia Feeny."

The receptionist ran a pale-polished fingernail down the computer screen, then looked up. "Mrs. Feeny's staying in 26B, but you'll probably find her in the common room. Follow that hallway to the end. It's the last door on the right."

"Thank you."

The tan-carpeted corridor led past numbered doors and bright floral prints. Trina stopped in front of a framed picture of a lilac bush to check her reflection in the glass. She must have used half a bottle of hairspray to keep any wisps from escaping the neat French braid, but she'd felt poised and assured at her interview. She might even pass her grandmother's inspection.

Residents' voices and canned music drifted from the common room. Trina hesitated in the doorway. A cluster of women and men stared at a game show on television. Two old ladies in wheelchairs sat with bright yarn and thick gray crochet hooks.

Grandma Olivia, her silver hair precisely parted and pinned in a bun, sat with a group playing cards at a table in the corner. They looked up as Trina approached.

Olivia let her cards fall from her gnarled hands. A tint of pink spread across her cheeks, and she cleared her throat twice before speaking. "Katrina! Friends, this is my granddaughter."

Trina gave her a quick hug, then stood back to be inspected.

Grandma Olivia clucked her tongue. "You're so thin! What do girls eat these days? And I'm sure you're not getting proper rest. Your hair's smart that way, dear, but it needs a good, short cut to control it. And that's a pretty dress—no doubt overpriced."

Trina kept her smile in place. The light in her grandmother's eyes said what the sharp critique tried to hide.

Grandma reached for her walker. "Let's find some place quiet to talk. They have the television turned up much too loud in here—for the old folks."

Trina matched her pace to her grandmother's shuffle. Anyone else would have subsided into a wheelchair by now, but not Grandma Olivia. Arthritis wouldn't win as long as her will could dominate her legs.

As they walked down the hall, Trina explained the job interview that had brought her to town and did her best to field her grandmother's rapid-fire questions. No, she wouldn't move in with her parents if she got the job. Yes, she was going to have supper with them tonight. No, she wasn't engaged yet.

"What about that young fellow you mentioned last time? Peter?"

Trina scuffed her shoes against the muted pattern of the carpet. "Pete's staying in Regina, where he works."

"Then why do you want to move back here?"

"Henderson's is a leader in graphic arts. This job would be a real boost to my career."

The older woman exhaled sharply. "Katrina, dear, why do you keep letting the good ones get away?"

Trina shook her head. "Grandma, I don't mind being single. The world won't end if I never get married." Maybe her teasing tone might sneak the truth past her grandmother's mental filters.

"When I was your age, I had children in school." Olivia led Trina into a small sitting room. "We can talk in here. Don't mind Estelle. She'll just sit there with that silly grin and hum to herself."

The little woman in the corner was smiling out the window and rocking in time to some internal music. A fluffy blue shawl lay across her lap, and she clutched a faded book on top of it.

Olivia slowly lowered herself onto a straight-back wooden chair. Trina drew up another seat and perched beside her.

Grandma kept Trina entertained for the better part of an hour with her opinions of the other residents. Sam MacDonald's new hip would fail if he didn't make more effort to walk. The nurses were too strict over Sally Trites's diet—a little chocolate never hurt anyone. And as for Wilfred Mills …

Olivia stopped to inspect the man who appeared in the doorway. He looked to be in his mid-fifties, and what hair remained was close-cropped and heavily grayed.

He waved a hand. "You ladies carry on. I'm here to see Estelle."

Grandma Olivia stiffened like a hunting dog catching a scent. "And who would *you* be?"

The newcomer's smile stayed in place as he limped over to them. "I'm Jeff Banks, Estelle's son."

Olivia studied his outstretched hand and sniffed. "I didn't know Estelle had any children. Your mother's been here for months without a single visitor." She appraised his worn but clean clothing. "She can't give you any money. It all goes for her keep."

"Grandma!" Trina flashed him an apologetic look, then turned to her grandmother. "Why don't you show me your room? I'm sure Mr. Banks and his mother would like to be alone."

"That's all right, miss." He gave her a lopsided grin. "I understand. And I'm glad Mother has folks here who care for her."

He glanced across the room at Estelle, then back to Olivia. "I've just finished a stint in the Arctic, and I'm looking for something that'll let me be nearer to Mother. I'm all the family she has left. And I've missed her."

"She's not even going to know you're here." Olivia didn't seem to notice the inconsistency of her arguments.

A patient smile creased Jeff Banks's face. "But I'll know."

In the corner, Estelle tilted her head, as if listening to a voice beyond their hearing, then clasped her hands and gave a secret little smile. Despite Estelle's mental state, the little woman radiated a quiet serenity.

Olivia sat straighter in her chair. "Pitiful—having to go on living when her mind's gone."

Trina squeezed her grandmother's knotted hand. A strong-willed woman like Olivia would fear loss of control most of all.

Jeff smiled. "Her mind isn't gone. It's just … at peace."

Olivia sniffed, but Trina was curious. "What do you mean?"

He snagged a wooden chair with his foot and sat on it. "Mother had a lot of hardship in her life. My father died young, and she raised me and my sisters alone. She did her best, but we were a handful. My younger sister drowned in her teens, and we lost my other sister to cancer not many years later."

Trina gasped. So much heartache. *And my biggest problem is a two-timing boyfriend.*

"I caused my share of grief too. But Mother knew I'd come back into the fold someday. She's been praying for me all these years." Tears glistened in his eyes. He got up from the chair and excused himself.

Trina couldn't let him go just yet. "Mr. Banks?"

He turned.

"How did she survive all that sorrow?"

"Whatever happened, she knew the Lord was with her, and she always trusted Him to take care of her." He ignored Olivia's disbelieving snort. "Look at her. Even now, when she's lost so much of herself, she has peace."

Trina glanced from Estelle to Olivia, each living the results of a lifetime's choices. Which was better off—the one who trusted a greater power, or the one who drove everybody nuts trying to maintain control?

And what about me? The sting of Pete's betrayal shot through Trina's stomach. Even a month later, she still felt like she was bleeding inside. "I'd like to believe there could be peace in the midst of pain." Had she actually said those words out loud?

"The Lord really does take care of us if we let Him." Jeff held her gaze for a moment. "It was a pleasure meeting you, ladies. God bless you both." He limped to his mother's side and knelt, cradling her withered hands in his work-worn ones.

Olivia stirred. "I faced all *my* troubles without religion. That's probably what addled the poor thing's brain."

She hoped Jeff hadn't heard that caustic remark.

Trina checked her watch. "Mom's expecting me in fifteen minutes. I have to scoot." She dropped a quick peck on her grandmother's leathery cheek. "Do you want to walk me to the door?"

"I've walked enough today. These old bones get tired, you know." Olivia's eyes lingered on Estelle and Jeff. Trina hoped she'd stay and soak in some of their calm spirit.

"I'll phone when I find out about the job." Trina paused, studying her grandmother's face. "I love you, Grandma."

Olivia's eyes brightened. "Make sure you get enough to eat. And try to find a nice young man."

"Don't worry, Grandma, I'll be fine. See you later."

Trina waved to Jeff, who still held Estelle's hand. "Have a nice day."

He grinned. "You too."

Trina exited the building. The sun-warmed grass sweetened the air, washing the institutional tang from her nostrils. Estelle's contented face lingered in her thoughts.

I'm not handling my pain very well on my own, God. If You're real, please show me how to find the peace that Jeff and his mother have.

Life Application

Most of us have someone in our lives who drives us a little bit crazy. We know Jesus wants us to love that person, and we do. But maintaining that relationship can feel like a custom-made lesson to test our patience.

We can set boundaries, and learn to respectfully articulate our frustrations, but few people are willing and able to see and address their flaws. And sometimes, what we see as a negative trait is viewed by the other person as a strength.

It's tempting to dwell on what irritates us to the point where resentment grows and we lose sight of what's genuinely lovable in a person. It can take a conscious act of will to choose to focus on the good. We may need to ask God to show us what He sees: tremendous potential in a soul He crafted and loves.

When I remember that I've occasionally needed forgiveness, patience, and grace from those around me, it's easier to extend the same to others. And when I realize how much Jesus has forgiven me for, I can then ask Him to love others through me.

About the Author

Janet Sketchley is the author of the Redemption's Edge novels. She blogs about faith and her books at janetsketchley.ca. She loves adventure stories, worship music, and tea. Fans of Christian suspense are invited to subscribe to Janet's monthly newsletter at bit.ly/JanetSketchleyNews.

6

Silk Roses

by Kathy Ide

Don't marry someone you can live with. Marry the man you can't live without.

As Jamie floated across the dance studio floor, her cousin Stacy's words of advice rang in her heart. She gazed into Tony's sparkling green eyes. He hadn't stopped looking at her since the waltz began. His arm around her waist, he led her gracefully through every turn and twirl.

This amazing man was definitely her soul mate. Tony made her feel loved. Cherished. Like she was the only woman in the world. Well, the only woman in *his* world.

"You're so beautiful," he whispered in her ear.

Her cheeks—already flushed from the dance—warmed even more.

Jamie's focus flitted back and forth between Tony's adorable face and the glittering diamond he'd placed on her finger on Valentine's Day one year ago. When they began making wedding plans, she'd shared her lifelong dream of dancing with her groom at the reception. His eyebrows rose, but after a moment's hesitation, he'd said, "If it's important to you, I'll learn." Just one of the many things Tony said that melted her heart.

The music ended, and Jamie reluctantly pulled out of her partner's arms. Soon they would share their first dance as Mr. and Mrs. Tony Thorpe. She could hardly wait.

"You all did splendidly." The dance instructor beamed at the six couples in the class. "Take a short breather, and then we'll end our session with a bunny hop."

As they rested their feet and quenched their thirst, Jamie thanked God yet again for bringing Tony into her life. She was so glad she'd followed her cousin's advice and saved herself for him. She'd dated a few nice guys, but never felt like any of them was "the one"—the one man she couldn't possibly live without. Not until Tony. The most romantic man on the face of the planet.

He was her forever love. Just like Stacy had found with her husband.

"Oh, darling, thanks again for taking dance lessons with me," Jamie cooed as Tony walked her to the door of her apartment.

He cupped her hand in his and brought it to his lips. "You know I'd do anything for you." He kissed her fingers. "Anything."

How many times could her heart melt before it became a puddle of mush? She wanted to spend a lifetime finding out.

When she fished the keys out of her purse, Tony took them. "Allow me." He unlocked her door.

The moment it cracked open, a powerful floral fragrance wafted out. Jamie's jaw dropped when she peered into her apartment.

Gorgeous flowers filled every inch of the room. Long-stemmed roses lay across the kitchen table. Vases of mixed arrangements sat on the counters. Jamie wondered where her knickknacks ended up.

"These must have cost a small fortune," she blurted out.

"You're worth every penny, and more." He tenderly kissed her lips. "But you don't want to talk about money on our engagement anniversary, do you, sweetheart?" His mouth hungrily devoured hers.

When his hands wandered, she gently redirected them. But they kept returning to her "forbidden zones."

"Tony," she murmured when he paused from kissing her.

"Shh." He tenderly touched her lips. "I want this night to be special." He swept her off her feet—literally—and headed toward the bedroom.

"Tony!" Shock and irritation shot through her. "Put me down. *Darling*."

"Oh, I will." He deposited her onto the bed.

Jamie popped to her feet. "What are you doing?"

He tucked a strand of hair behind her ear. "Celebrating Valentine's Day with the woman I'll love forever."

"But we vowed to stay pure until we got married."

He caressed her cheek. "You're already my bride. We've committed our lives to each other in the sight of God. In Bible days, an engagement was as binding as a marriage."

She took a step back. "But the betrothed couple was not to … you know … participate in the ways that lead to children."

He grinned. "Don't worry. I'll make sure you don't get pregnant." He reached to embrace her. She stepped back again—too quickly—and flopped onto her back on the bed.

His grin broadened. "That's my girl."

He lunged for her, but she rolled over and stood, leaving him sprawled out on her grandmother's quilt. "Tony, I … I think you need to leave."

He grabbed her wrist and pulled her on top of him. "I think you need to lighten up."

Jamie struggled to escape his strong grip. How could the sweet man she'd fallen in love with turn so quickly into a pushy attacker? Was this an isolated incident? Or an indication of how he'd treat her after they were married?

When she finally broke free, she yelled, "Get out of my house. And … and don't come back!"

Tony stood, adjusting his clothes. "I'm glad I found out now what a prude you are."

Prude?

He extended his palm. "I want the ring back."

"What?"

"I'm gonna need it to pay for all those useless flowers. They're not cheap, you know."

Jamie twisted the ring, trying to get it past her knuckle. "And how *were* you planning to pay for them?"

"Same way I've financed everything I've bought you. Credit cards."

"Which would become my bills after we were married."

He shrugged. "What's mine is yours, baby. And what's yours … is mine." He leered at her body.

Jamie wrenched the ring off her finger and threw it at him. He caught it like a professional baseball player.

"Thanks for understanding," Jamie told her coworker on the phone.

"No problem," Rick said. "You sound awful."

"I just had a really rough Valentine's Day." That was putting it mildly. "I might need a few days to … recover." Jamie hadn't seen her cousin since she moved to Missouri after her wedding five years ago. She couldn't wait to see Stacy. And wasn't sure she'd want to leave.

"Well, take as much time off as you need. I'll let the boss know you're sick, and we'll hold down the fort till you're up to coming back."

"I really appreciate it."

"Hope you feel better soon." Rick worked in the sales department, so Jamie didn't know him that well. But he'd always seemed nice.

"So, how was *your* Valentine's Day?" she asked.

"Same as any other day. Except the pizza delivery guy arrived in record time." He chuckled.

Jamie stared at her cousin across the kitchen table. "What do you mean you're divorced?"

Stacy shrugged. "Just didn't work out after all."

"But you said he was the one man in the world you couldn't live without."

She stared into her steaming cup of cinnamon tea. "Living *with* him turned out to be a whole lot worse."

Jamie studied her cousin's face. Her smooth forehead now creased with furrows. The deep crinkles around her eyes. The edges of her lips curved down. "But divorce? Stacy, my pastor says—"

"He hit me, Jame. Constantly told me how stupid and ugly I am. Came home drunk after spending hours in bars, proposing to topless waitresses."

Jamie's breaths came in gulps. "Not Brad. He was so charming. So sweet." So much like Tony.

"Why do you think I fell in love with him? And thought he was 'the one'? It wasn't till after I married him that the nightmare started."

Jamie took a sip of her vanilla chai. Would the same thing have happened if she'd married Tony?

"I was wrong." Stacy took Jamie's trembling fingers into her hands. "Don't marry the man you think you can't live without. Marry someone you can live with … for the rest of your life."

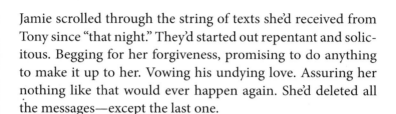

Jamie scrolled through the string of texts she'd received from Tony since "that night." They'd started out repentant and solicitous. Begging for her forgiveness, promising to do anything to make it up to her. Vowing his undying love. Assuring her nothing like that would ever happen again. She'd deleted all the messages—except the last one.

My love, please come back to me. I can't go on without you. I don't know what I might do if I can't have you.

Was there a warning in those words? Even a threat?

This time, Tony's romantic effusions didn't melt Jamie's heart. They now seemed contrived, even manipulative.

Even before Jamie turned the key in the lock of her apartment, the putrid odor from inside assaulted her. When she opened the door, the sight and smell turned her stomach. Dead, wilted flowers lay everywhere. Gooey stems drooped over vases. Brown buds dotted the counters. Wrinkled petals covered the carpet.

Holding her hand over her nose and mouth, Jamie shuffled across the floor, trying to avoid squishing any of the goopy mess into the carpet and making a permanent stain.

After brushing aside a few chunks of brittle baby's breath, Jamie collapsed onto the couch and stared at the disaster. How could something so lovely turn into something so nauseating in a matter of days?

Returning to the office was the last thing Jamie felt like doing. But if she didn't force herself to get out of the house, she'd spend all day crying and feeling sorry for herself.

She walked into work a few minutes late. No one seemed to notice her bloodshot eyes or the catch in her voice. If they did, they probably attributed them to lingering symptoms of her alleged illness.

As she rounded the corner of her cubicle wall, she saw a small white vase with six red roses sitting on her desk. The yellow sticky note attached to the vase said, *Sorry you had a crummy Valentine's Day.*

She drew closer and inhaled—but no floral scent exuded from the blooms.

"They're silk."

Jamie whirled around and saw Rick.

"I wasn't sure when you'd be back, so I got something that'd still look nice whenever you came in."

"That's very thoughtful. Thanks."

"You feeling better?"

Jamie thought about it for a minute. "Actually, I am."

"I hope you don't mind not getting fresh flowers."

Jamie shuddered at the thought of the mess she'd spent hours cleaning up. "I actually like these better. A lot better."

His brow rose. "You do?"

"Yeah. These will last. Forever."

"If you feel up to it, maybe we could get some dinner after work." He grinned. "I know a place that serves delicious chicken-noodle soup."

Jamie laughed. "That sounds great. But I have …" Dance lesson night? She no longer had a wedding reception to practice for. "I have …" A bad breakup to get over? What better way to do that than to enjoy a relaxing evening with a guy who wouldn't pressure her into anything?

"I have … an intense craving for something more substantial than soup."

His eyes lit up. "They serve a mouth-watering sirloin."

"Sounds perfect."

Life Application

Flittering emotions can set relationships on a tumbling roller-coaster ride of euphoric highs and devastating lows, making us dizzy and sick. But God's love is steady, unchanging, and unfailing. His affection for you will never fade, wilt, or die. And His love is perfect—just as He is perfect.

God loves each of us in a unique, special way. He delights in you. He wants to wrap an arm around your waist, take your hand, and dance with you. If you let Him lead, He will direct you into paths of love, joy, and peace. In the midst of life's most difficult circumstances, He can make you feel like you're floating on clouds. If you focus on

Him. On His face. And on the perfect love that flows from His heart into yours.

He is the only one You can't live without.

About the Author

Kathy Ide, author of *Proofreading Secrets of Best-Selling Authors,* is a freelance editor/mentor for new writers, established authors, and book publishers. She speaks at writers' conferences across the country. She is also the founder and director of The Christian PEN and the Christian Editor Connection. For more, visit KathyIde.com.

7

My Hero

by Marci Seither

"Mom!"

Kate Wakefield's seven-year-old daughter's voice echoed in the bathroom down the hall. Kate sighed. The last thing she needed was to have her teething eighteen-month-old's bedtime ritual interrupted by his sister's overdramatic yelling.

"Mom!" Alyson wailed again, even louder.

After tucking Max's soft blanket around him, Kate rushed to the blue-and-yellow bathroom, where Alyson and five-year-old Tobey were supposed to be getting ready for bed. "What's going on in here?"

"He dropped the toothpaste in the toilet!"

The sleeve of Tobey's pajamas was drenched. The dripping toothpaste tube held between his wet fingers told the story.

"Sorry." Tobey's blue eyes were wide with anticipation of being reprimanded. A blue-and-white-striped bath towel lay on the floor, where he had apparently tried to wipe up some of the water. "It was an accident."

"Do I have to use that?" Alyson put her hands on her hips.

Kate took a deep breath. "Go in my bathroom, honey, and get the extra tube from my drawer. But be quiet about it."

Alyson skipped down the hall.

Kate looked at her watch. "I sure wish your daddy would get home." With a huge graphic design package due in a few days for her biggest customer, Kate needed a few calm hours to meet the deadline.

She took the wet toothpaste from Tobey's outstretched hand and dropped it in the wastepaper basket. She helped him peel off his pajama top, plopping it on the floor next to the towel.

Good thing I don't have a real job, Kate thought sarcastically. Having been in the corporate world before she and Dan got married, Kate was used to dressing in dry-clean-only suits and eating at nice restaurants every week. When they welcomed their first child into the world, Kate exchanged her high-heeled pumps and tailored wardrobe for tennis shoes and denim jeans. She didn't regret the decision. But after juggling motherhood and freelancing all day, she fell into bed most nights completely exhausted.

"Where is Daddy?" asked Tobey.

"He had a business dinner." Kate bit back a sting of jealousy.

When Alyson returned, Kate helped her open the new tube and squeezed a small bead of creamy white paste onto the little toothbrushes. When she heard a car pulling into the garage, she smiled. "If you get to bed right after you finish brushing, I'll bet Daddy will read you a story before you go to sleep."

The kitchen door opened. "Where's my family?"

The kids spit into the sink, then ran out to greet him.

"Quietly," Kate reminded them.

When she rounded the corner, she saw both kids in Dan's strong arms. "And how is my lovely wife?" He gave Kate a wink.

"After three loads of laundry, fishing toothpaste out of the toilet, and finding out that Alyson needs to bring homemade cookies to a bake sale in two days, the fact that the house is still standing means it was a good day!" Kate picked up a few plastic blocks and a stuffed elephant that sang whenever someone squeezed its trunk and put them in the basket next to the couch. "How was your business meeting?"

"It was fine, except for running long. But what else is new?"

Kate started loading the dishwasher. Dan put the kids down, sent them to pick out a book for him to read, then walked up to Kate and wrapped his arms around her waist. She relaxed into his embrace.

"If I'm not mistaken, we have an anniversary coming up in a few weeks," he whispered. "What should we do to celebrate?"

Kate sighed. "I can't even think about that right now."

Dan kissed the side of her neck. "How about after I get our little critters tucked in bed?"

Kate gave Dan a sheepish look. "I have a deadline. I need to work late again tonight."

Dan gently kissed her lips. "I'll wait up." He disappeared down the hall.

Kate checked on Max before going to her office at the far end of the house. She worked until her eyes felt the fatigue of looking at a computer screen for hours on end. When she checked her watch, she discovered it was after midnight.

She shut down everything and crept toward her room. The bedside light was off. After changing into her nightgown and brushing her teeth, she slid between the covers. Her muscles relaxed against the soft cotton sheets. The sound of Dan's deep breathing lulled her to sleep.

When the alarm chirped to life, Dan rolled over. "I waited up for you as long as I could." His fingertips caressed her bare arm.

"Sorry. I lost track of time."

He kissed her, then rolled out of bed. Kate headed to the kitchen and turned on the coffeepot.

Dan entered the room, dressed in his suit and tie. "So, what's on the agenda for your day?"

"I have Bible study this morning." Kate poured the fragrant coffee into two big mugs and handed one to Dan.

"Have a great time." He picked up his briefcase, kissed her quickly, and headed out the door.

As Kate watched the car leave the driveway, her eyes pooled with tears.

We used to be spontaneous and fun. Now we're busy and tired. Kate stared out the window. The small potted geranium at the edge of the porch had dropped most of its red petals, and only a couple of leaves clung to the thin stem. *Is that what our marriage looks like?*

A few hours later, Kate had managed to get all the kids dressed, fed, and to church. They loved being with their friends and always did a fun craft together while their moms enjoyed the Bible study.

The group leader, Stacy, read a passage from Song of Solomon about the ways a husband and wife should relate to each other.

"In the busyness of everyday life, sometimes we forget to make time for our spouses," she said. "It's easy to fall in love when there are few distractions. But staying in love is a choice. It takes commitment and focus, but it's worth it. Because once the kids are gone, you'll only have each other. We need to make our marriages a priority, no matter how crazy busy our lives get."

All the way home, Kate thought about the many things she loved about Dan. In so many little everyday ways, he really was her hero. And Stacy was right. Good marriages didn't just happen. They needed tending, just like the geranium on her porch.

"Something smells delicious," Dan said as he walked into the kitchen.

Kate finished setting the table for dinner. "Enchiladas."

Dan grinned. "My favorite."

"I know." She pulled the hot pan out of the oven.

As the family sat around the table, Max played in his high chair while Alyson showed Dan the craft she made during Kate's Bible study. Tobey rolled up his sleeve to reveal the stick-on Spiderman tattoo on his upper arm—a body decoration he'd received at a superhero-themed birthday party the day before. He went into great detail about how it was put on with wet paper towels at room temperature, and promised it would wash off the next time he took a shower.

After dinner, Kate told Dan, "I have a few more things to take care of for my client tonight." She winked. "But after you read to the kids, you can wait up for me."

He grinned and wiggled his eyebrows.

Kate pushed the Send button on her last e-mail at ten o'clock. After shutting down the computer, she practically skipped toward the bedroom. She passed their wedding portrait that hung in the hall. Dan was still the most attractive man she'd ever met.

She opened the door. Dan's deep breathing told her he was sound asleep. As she neared the bed, she noticed the top sheet covered most of his body—all but his naked bum. All at once, a silly idea popped into her mind.

Stifling a giggle, Kate slipped out of the bedroom and tiptoed to Tobey's room. Rifling through his box of temporary superhero tattoos, she found the perfect one. Flash Gordon.

Trying not to burst into laughter, she ran a few paper towels under body-temperature water. *This definitely counts for being spontaneous!*

When the alarm sounded the next morning, Kate looked over at Dan. "I came to bed early, but you were already asleep."

"Yeah, right." Dan wrapped a robe around him and headed toward the closet.

"But I did," Kate said coyly. "And I have proof."

Dan turned around. "What are you talking about?"

She winked. "Go to the mirror and check your backside."

Finally releasing her giggles, Kate scurried to the kitchen to start breakfast. Along the way, she noticed the neglected plant. After putting on her sweater, she went outside with a pitcher of water.

Dan came outside, his cheeks colored with a faint pinkish glow. "What are you doing?"

"Just a little nurturing. Of this plant … and of my husband." Kate wrapped her arms around Dan's neck. "Or should I say 'my hero'?"

Life Application

It's easy to get distracted and focus on things other than our mates. Even good things, like friendship, church activities, and kids can take precedence over our spouses. As moms, we feel pulled in many directions. There's carpool, homework, music lessons, dance recitals, soccer practice, and the list goes on. But it's important to remember that our husbands come first.

When I was a young mom, my mother told me to take time to enjoy my husband's company and continue to work on our relationship, even amidst the business of raising a family. I've always treasured that advice.

Philippians 2:3–4 says, "Do nothing out of selfish ambition or vain conceit. Rather, in humility value others above yourselves, not looking to your own interests but each of you to the interests of the others."

While this verse isn't necessarily about marriage, the truth rings true for couples. Putting your spouse first, above everything except God, isn't always easy, but it is vital to a successful long-term relationship. Like a geranium, love needs to be watered to keep growing.

About the Author

Marci Seither has been married to John for thirty years. They are the parents of six kiddos who have provided her with volumes of adventure, symphonies of laughter, and loads of laundry. She has written hundreds of articles, including op/eds, feature stories, and human-interest. She has authored two books: *Empty Nest: Strategies to Help Your Kids Take Flight* and *The Adventures of Pearley Monroe*.

8

God Spelled Backwards

by Rachel Barrett

Blair slammed down the hood of her car. *Great. Just great.* She restrained an urge to kick the cantankerous beast and slipped into the front seat to gather her purse and scarf. Maybe her new boss wouldn't mind a dead metal dinosaur parked front and center at the office over the weekend. Until she found a good mechanic, she'd be walking.

She gritted her teeth and hopped out, burrowing her hands deep into her coat pockets. Icy slush from yesterday's snow crunched under her shoes as she stepped onto the crosswalk. Dampness seeped through the imitation leather that was supposed to be waterproof.

Tires hummed on the slick pavement as passing cars spat fine muddy spray. Every boutique window flaunted gaudy paper-heart displays and garish signs boasting the latest diamond ring sale. And it wasn't even February yet. Blair tore her gaze away. Cheerful frills, true love, and warm fuzzies didn't extend to divorcées or recent transfers to this town. Maybe if she pretended hard enough, the whole Valentine's season would just slip right on by. She wondered if loneliness could choke a person.

A scritch-scratch on the pavement behind her caught her attention. Something moving. *Someone?* She wheeled to confront it.

Woof!

Blair looked down at her stalker—one wet, skinny, bedraggled puppy. She smiled in relief, and the poor thing perked up with a yip.

This town seemed to be the drop-off point for every abandoned stray in three counties. This one had been on its own for a while, that was certain.

Recalling the remains of her lunch, Blair dug into her satchel. The shivering little dog snuffled eagerly, holding up one slush-drenched paw. Blair knelt and offered the half sandwich. It disappeared in one gulp, and a wet nose nudged her fingers for more.

"Sorry, pup, you're out of luck." She showed her empty hands. "Better hit the road." She turned for home and didn't look back.

Ten blocks had never felt so long as her numb feet carried her to the door of her new apartment. Kicking the snow from her ruined shoes, she stepped inside. *Thank You, God, for space heaters.* What a stroke of foresight to have left it running that morning. The landlord might get the central heating fixed by July. Or not.

A piteous whine caught her up short. A furry face pleaded outside the glass patio door as a wagging stub tail proclaimed the eternal faith of puppyhood.

Blair sighed, recalling tonight's forecast for more snow. And the apartment was lonely.

She opened the door. "All right, come on." The puppy trotted in and gave a mighty shake, flinging drops of muddy snow. Blair dashed for a towel. "But just one night, understand?"

Hearing sounds of battle, Blair peeked into the tiny den, where everything she hadn't needed in the three weeks since she moved in had ended up. Shredded cardboard boxes. Packing peanuts strewn helter-skelter. And one puppy wearing the world champion of innocent faces.

She muffled a sigh and knelt to gather the pieces. No use saying "bad dog" now. "I'm going to need to give you a lot of grace, aren't I?" The furry little rascal's eager tail-wagging confirmed it. "Guess I'll just have to call you Gracie then."

The pup yipped cheerfully until Blair burst into laughter.

Fending off Gracie's earnest efforts to help, Blair shoved the last few pieces into a plastic garbage bag. Then she swooped up the wiggling bundle and sashayed into the hall to the swinging beat of "I Heart You" playing on the radio.

Gracie licked madly at her chin. A husband who'd gotten tired of being married and coworkers who only wanted to talk about their love lives didn't even blip on Blair's radar anymore.

One little black-and-white ball of energy with soulful eyes and perky ears had overshadowed all that.

Maybe this Valentine's season wouldn't be so heart-crushing after all.

Clutching Gracie in one arm, Blair dumped the bag of cardboard bits into the recycle bin. A kibble-powered chipper-shredder could actually be quite handy, come to think of it. She'd always hated breaking boxes apart.

Passing the bookshelf, she glimpsed her Bible, dusty and half hidden behind a pile of self-help books. Her conscience poked her, and she looked away. How long had it been since she'd cracked it open? Or gone to church?

One of these days. She still listened to the local radio devotional every morning. Yesterday's had been on stewardship, hadn't it? Something about what we do with the things God gives us to take care of. Right now, Gracie needed all the time Blair could spare.

She plopped her charge on the living room rug and headed for the kitchen. If she remembered correctly, a cupid cookie cutter was lurking somewhere in the cabinet. And Valentine's Day was just around the corner.

Gracie barked furiously, pawing at the front door. Dusting flour off her hands, Blair went over. "What's the matter, girl?"

The pup peered out the window, nose to the cold pane.

"There's nothing there, silly." But Gracie wouldn't stop whimpering. Blair opened the door a crack to make sure.

A flash of yellow fur darted out from the patio hedge. With a yelp Gracie squeezed through the doorway and raced after the cat.

"Gracie, no!" Ignoring Blair's stern command, cat and dog streaked down the sidewalk.

She grabbed her coat and keys and dashed out into the snow. Half a block away, the puppy slalomed around the corner and disappeared.

"Gracie, come back!" Blair sprinted as fast as the slippery pavement would allow. When she reached the corner, panting and shivering, the road was empty.

Street lamps blinked through tumbling snowflakes, lighting the sidewalk just enough for Blair to pick her way around the deepest drifts. She smeared away tears and tried to rub some feeling back into her face.

Hunched against the chill, Blair crossed the street toward her apartment. How many hours had she been walking? Staying out any longer seemed futile.

She returned home and headed straight for the bathroom. After waiting for the water to go from frigid to tepid, she stepped into the shower.

Her arms and legs burned as feeling slowly returned. Cursing the apartment's pathetic excuse for a water heater, she turned off the lukewarm flow, toweled dry, and threw on socks and a bathrobe. Huddled under a blanket on the couch, she mopped fresh tears with her flannel sleeve.

The radio playing softly in the kitchen grated on her. Some pastor was preaching a sermon about "the greatest Valentine ever given—in the shape of a cross."

Blair tried to squash the nagging voice in her head that asked if she had stopped just once, all afternoon, to pray about her missing dog. She threw off the blanket, stomped into the kitchen, and punched the power button on the radio. Silence was better than that drivel.

She snagged her satchel from the back of the couch. There should be a tissue in there somewhere. Fishing in the depths, she located the plastic packet. But it snared on something in the disordered contents of her bag. With a jerk, it finally popped free, flipping out a stiff little crumple of paper. Blair blew her nose, wadded the tissue, and picked up the paper.

It was a photograph. Gracie's winsome face peered out at her, nose almost touching the camera as her tongue reached out to slobber on the lens. Blair gently smoothed away the creases.

The picture blurred in her vision and she swiped at her eyes. *I thought You gave her to me, God.* She blinked and sniffled. *Why did You take her away?*

Tears flowed, faster than her sleeve could handle, and she buried her face in the fuzzy blanket. The picture dropped to the carpet.

Something scratched at the door. Blair froze.

A faint whine spurred her off the couch, and she stumbled over her own feet getting to the entryway. When she yanked the door open, a trembling, sodden, whimpering dog scrambled into her arms.

"Gracie!" Blair caught her up and squeezed. Shutting the door against the freezing air, she clutched the shivering puppy tight to her chest and buried her face in wet fur. *Thank You, thank You, thank You.*

Blair dried the pup with a towel, then knelt beside the space heater to thaw out her popsicle paws. Gracie cuddled into her shoulder and Blair rocked her like a baby. "I don't care where you went. I'm just glad you came home."

The words seemed to echo in Blair's heart. Her gaze fell on the dusty Bible.

It was time she came home too.

Life Application

God speaks into our lives in many ways, especially through relationships—even the love of a pet. He promises, "You will seek Me and find Me, when you search for Me with all your heart" (Jeremiah 29:13 NKJV). Even when we chase after the cares of this world and wander away, getting hopelessly lost, He never gives up on us. "I have loved you with an everlasting love; therefore with lovingkindness I have drawn you" (Jeremiah 31:3 NKJV).

Just as the compassionate father welcomed his prodigal son home with rejoicing and celebration, so our merciful Lord will do for each one of us.

About the Author

Rachel Barrett writes clean Westerns and lives in the Chihuahuan Desert with her husband, Paul, where they raise dwarf goats and velociraptors—er, chickens. When she's not out with her horses, attempting another crazy stunt involving high speeds and the Lone Ranger theme song, she's usually crouched over her keyboard, feverishly typing a new story. She blogs at ranchitobandito.wordpress.com.

9

Desert Crossing

by Dona Watson

*L*ori lowered herself into her office chair and stared at the computer screen. Her fingers trembled over the keyboard, her fear too thick to type in the address to the sheriff's website one more time. But Josh hadn't come home again last night and she needed answers.

Taking a deep breath, she clicked the link for yesterday's arrest log and scanned down the list of names, looking for her son's. There it was, halfway down the list. Joshua Coleville. She shut her eyes tight against the tears that would not be denied.

"God, why?" Lori's heart felt as dry and cracked as an empty lake bed. Dealing with Josh had drained her, and she didn't know how much longer she could keep going.

The first time her son was arrested for possession of heroin, he'd called her from jail. As much as it pained her, she had refused to pick him up. She hated to say it, but when he was in jail, as least she knew where he was. That was better than him lying in a dirty alley somewhere dying of a drug overdose.

She pushed away from the desk and stumbled into the family room, her heart aching. She and David had such high hopes when their son was born. The first time she looked down into his tiny face, she'd whispered, "Little Joshua. Someday you'll be a great man of God, just like Joshua in the Bible." But her son had turned away from God and spent all his time either high or making a deal that would ensure his next fix.

She scooped up a framed 5x7 of her husband and traced the lines of his face, the glass cool against her fingertips. David looked so handsome in his dress uniform, his eyes bright with the playful spark that had attracted her to him the first time they'd met. She wondered where he was today. Probably somewhere in the hot desert sands of the Middle East, maybe Afghanistan. He wasn't always allowed to say where.

She reached for a tissue and wiped at the river of tears running down her cheeks. "Oh, David. I wish you were here. You'd know what to do."

It had been hard to raise a teenage boy with her husband deployed overseas. Soon after Josh graduated from high school, he started hanging out with the wrong crowd.

Lori clutched the photo to her chest and felt herself sinking into the dark pit of depression she had been trying so hard to escape from. She drifted off into a restless sleep filled with dreams of what might have been.

A key in the front door rattled Lori from her dark slumber. She jolted up, her heart thumping in alarm.

"Josh?" Her fingers trembled so much, she nearly dropped the framed photo in her attempt to put it back on the end table. In the next room, heavy footsteps crossed the wood floor. She sat up, trying to blink away groggy clouds of sleep. Across the darkened bedroom, the clock read 11:30.

The browns and greens of an army combat uniform stepped through the door. Lori rubbed at her eyes, certain it was a hallucination. When she looked again, she saw David placing his bag on the floor, a weary smile on his face.

Lori choked out a sob. Throwing herself into her husband's arms, she buried her face in his shoulder.

David held her tight for several moments, then stepped back and held her at arm's length. "I've been dreaming of this moment for thousands of miles."

"But … you're not supposed to be here!"

The twinkle that she loved crept into his eyes. "Should I leave?"

Lori pulled him back into her arms, savoring the feel and taste of his lips. For several minutes they stood holding each other. "You must be exhausted. Or hungry. Let me get you something to eat." She pulled him to the kitchen.

He sat at the breakfast bar and Lori went to the refrigerator, pulling out the foil container of lasagna she'd ordered from the deli the night before and then didn't feel like eating.

As she scooped the pasta onto a plate, David asked, "Is Josh upstairs? I can't wait to see him."

Lori stopped, took a deep breath, and faced her husband. But words couldn't have been further away.

His forehead creased in a frown. "What's wrong?"

"Josh …" Her voice caught. "Josh is in jail."

David's eyebrows raised.

Lori ran her thumb along the edge of the counter. "He's been struggling since you left. Started doing drugs a few months ago."

"Drugs?" David whooshed out a breath.

"I tried to convince him to get help, but he refused. Just kept saying he wasn't that bad. That he could stop anytime he wanted." Lori bit her lip to keep it from trembling. "I'm sorry, David. Maybe I could have done something differently—"

"Shh." He stood, wrapped his arms around her, and kissed the top of her head. "I'm sure you did all you could. Don't take this on yourself." He pulled back, fire in his eyes. "But when I get a hold of that kid …"

Lori put her hands on her husband's cheeks. "There's something you need to hear." She led him to the kitchen table and told him about Josh's lying and stealing money from her purse, how she'd told Josh that if he got caught and went to jail, she wouldn't bail him out.

David took her hands. "Good for you. Sounds like he's right where he needs to be."

Leaving David deep in thought, Lori went back to the task of heating the lasagna in the microwave. David ate every bite as she continued catching him up. Then they snuggled on the couch and talked long into the night.

Sometime after two a.m., Lori fell asleep on David's shoulder. When the sun's rays shone through the window onto her face, she awoke to the scent of eggs and coffee.

She pushed aside the afghan David had wrapped around her sometime in the night. Stretching, she shuffled into the kitchen to find her husband scattering cubes of cheddar into a pan of steaming scrambled eggs.

"Morning, beautiful. Hungry?"

Lori nodded. Though her heart was still heavy with thoughts of Josh, for the first time in days, she actually did feel hungry. David divided the eggs onto two plates while Lori popped bread into the toaster. They had just sat down, held hands, and blessed the food when the front door opened and then softly clicked shut.

"Josh," Lori called out. "Would you please come here for a moment?"

The nineteen-year-old shuffled to the doorway and leaned one shoulder against the frame. Dark circles ringed bloodshot eyes. But when Josh's gaze landed on his father, recognition lit up his face. "Dad!"

"Hello, Son." Despite David's harsh words from the night before, the husky tone in his voice spoke only of a father's love. "Where've you been?"

He hung his head and mumbled, "I'm guessing you already know. I screwed up, Dad."

David stood and opened his arms. But Josh took a step back. "I have to say something to Mom before I lose my nerve." He looked at his shoes. "I thought about a lot of things when I was in jail." He lifted his gaze. "You were right. I need help. I don't want to be locked up the rest of my life."

David crossed the kitchen and wrapped his son in a fierce embrace. "It takes a real man to admit when he needs help."

Tears of joy blurred Lori's vision and she joined her family. Rough days still lay ahead, but at least now there was hope.

As she breathed a prayer of thanks, the words her pastor had quoted in Sunday's sermon echoed in her mind. "I will open rivers on the bare heights, and fountains in the midst of the valleys. I will make the wilderness a pool of water, and the dry land springs of water" (Isaiah 41:18 ESV).

The dry cracks in the desert that once had been Lori's heart began to heal.

Life Application

Have the burdens of life worn you down so far that you can't see any rescue in sight? Those are the times when God loves to step in and shower us with cool rain that encourages and refreshes our souls. God has promised that when we walk through valleys so dark we can't see what's ahead, He'll be there. When we find ourselves at the end of our strength, He will hold our hands and see us through to the other side. The hard times and difficult situations might not go away, but He offers us fountains of cool water springing from the depths of His love.

Won't you rest today in the comfort of His arms? You are His treasure, His precious jewel. His true love.

About the Author

Dona Watson grew up with books and an imagination full of mystery and adventure. Her fantasy novel, *The Lightstone of Perlan,* placed in two contests, and her short stories have been published online and in print. You can find her at home in Southern California surrounded by way too many books or online at www.donawatson.com.

10

For the Love of Peter

by Marsha Hubler

Will be home Saturday next.

Hannah Stoltzfus read the text message that had just popped up on her phone. Hunched behind a stack of hay bales in the barn on her family's farm, the eighteen-year-old focused on the message from the love of her life, and her heart almost pounded out of her chest.

"Peter's coming home after two years," she whispered to Samson, the buggy horse munching on sweet feed a few feet away. "Maybe now Daed will grant him my hand in marriage."

Hannah peeked around the hay and spotted her father outside the barn, hitching Butch and Big Red, humongous sorrel shires, to the plow. April's sunshine had melted the central Pennsylvania snow, and planting season now called the Old Older Amish to their fields.

Hannah watched every move her daed made as he slapped the reins on the horses' backsides and steered his plow toward the south fields. She released a sigh. If Daed, or Mamm for that matter, knew she had a cell phone, they'd be madder than a bull with his horns caught in the fence. She'd be brought before the Ordnung's council to confess her wicked sin and repent. So would her best friend, Rachel Burkholder, who charged a pocketful of phones three times a week at English homes where she cleaned.

Oh, there were numerous Amish teens who had phones out in the open, but they had declared their *Rumschpringe* and left home, like Peter Brunheiller had. Some would return to the community, join the church, and be saved from eternal torment. Others would seek the ways of the world and be doomed to hell. Surely Peter would make the right choice.

When Peter headed to Scranton to work for a house painting contractor, half of Hannah's heart had gone with him. But the other half still clung to Amish tradition and, most of all, to her family. She couldn't imagine ever walking away from her faith and never seeing them again.

Hannah snuck toward the open barn door and peered out, spotting Mamm hoeing the garden. *Where I should be right this minute!* With Hannah's six siblings still in school, Mamm needed all the help she could get.

A barely audible jingle brought Hannah back to the phone. A text from Peter!

Have something urgent to tell you. Life changed for the better. Will look for you at the hymn sing.

Tell me now, Hannah messaged back. As she waited for a response, her mother headed straight toward her. Hannah clicked off her phone, pulled a handkerchief from her apron pocket, wrapped the phone in the hanky, and shoved the wad back into her apron.

"What do you need?" Hannah asked.

"The rake and spade. We'll have no trouble filling a wheelbarrow with rocks."

"I'll get them and be right there."

"*Danke*," Mamm said and hurried back to the garden.

Retrieving the tools, Hannah's nerves quivered. "This is stupid," she told herself. "I should just leave on my *Rumschpringe* and be done with it." Katie was doing all right, living in an apartment in Williamsport and cleaning for the English. And she'd said Hannah could live with her.

But she had to be at home when Peter came back for good.

Saturday at sunset, in Jake and Martha Laudenseller's barn, Hannah, Rachel, and all the courting-age girls sat on two rows of hay bales, facing two rows of eligible bachelors in their monthly hymn sing. Using the Ausbund, the traditional German hymnal, they sang hymns a capella in four-part harmony. In the yard, a dozen parents prepared refreshments for the two-hour event.

"I don't see Peter," Rachel whispered, her blue eyes scanning the room. "Maybe he couldn't come after all."

"He said he'd be here." Hannah's heart plummeted. She hadn't heard from him in three days.

"Oh, Hannah, I hope he wasn't in an accident."

"Now, turn to number fifty-three." Mr. Laudenseller paged through his hymnal, and for the next hour, the young people sang. But Peter never came.

Long after dark, the young people headed to the refreshment tables illuminated by kerosene lamps dotting the yard. As Hannah and Rachel filed out, a strange hissing sound distracted them.

"What was that?" Rachel asked.

Hannah turned, squinted at the corner of the barn, and saw Peter peeking out. He motioned for her to come.

"What's he doing?" Rachel whispered.

"I don't know. Go join the others. I'll find out."

Rachel hurried away, and Hannah darted behind the barn. As she stood face-to-face with the boy she had loved ever since he gave her a fistful of bluebells in first grade, her heart ached to fall into his arms.

"Why are you hiding?" she asked.

He took her hands in his. "Hannah, you've been on my mind every minute of every day. I love you more than life itself. That's why I needed to see you … to tell you in person."

"Tell me what?"

"I'm not coming back."

Hannah's knees weakened, and she felt like she was going to faint. "Have you … found another girl?"

He chuckled. "It's nothing like that. Hannah, I have accepted Christ as my personal Savior. A man I work with invited me to his church a few weeks ago, and he said things

I never heard before. The Ordnung's rules and the church's edicts won't get us into heaven."

Hannah stared at Peter. "You aren't making sense."

"As much as it breaks my heart, I must say good-bye to my family and friends." Tears flooded Peter's eyes.

He shoved an envelope into her hand. "My English friend helped me choose some verses for you to read. Please look at them and pray to Gott that He'll show you the truth. I want you to be my wife. But even more, I want you to accept Christ into your life and have the joy of knowing you'll go to heaven one day."

Tears trickled down Hannah's face. "I … I don't know what to—"

"I must go, my love." He brushed a tear from her cheek. "Please text me after you've studied the Scriptures and let me know your decision. If you accept Gott's truths, I will come for you. If you decide against it … I will never stop praying for you."

Hannah peeked at the yard to see if anyone was watching. When she turned back, Peter was gone.

Hannah dimmed the lamp in her bedroom and read what Peter had written. She grabbed her Bible from the nightstand, flopped onto her bed, and found the verses he'd said had changed his life. Strange verses she'd never heard preached from the Amish pulpit.

"For the wages of sin is death; but the gift of God is eternal life through Jesus Christ our Lord" (Romans 6:23 KJV).

"By grace are ye saved through faith; and that not of your-selves: it is the gift of God: not of works, lest any man should boast" (Ephesians 2:8–9 KJV).

For hours, Hannah read and reread Peter's letter and the Bible verses. She prayed and wept, agonizing over what Peter said was truth. And her love for a man she wasn't sure she even knew. And the life-changing decisions she had to make.

If I leave, I'll never see my family again.
If I leave, Peter will expect me to believe as he does.
How can these verses be true?
Is the Ordnung wrong?
Gott, please show me the way.

Hannah spent the worst month of her life, praying through sleepless nights, withdrawing into deep thought, and telling everyone who asked that "nothing was the matter."

During one Sunday morning meeting, as Preacher Martin spoke about the only way to heaven being obedience to the rules of the Ordnung, Hanna thought about those Bible verses Peter sent her. The Lord spoke to her through His holy Word, and she made her decision.

In the barn that afternoon, she pulled out her phone and texted Peter.

I have repented of my sins and asked Christ to be my Savior.
A tremendous burden has been lifted from my soul. Now I know

I have eternal life and don't have to worry about working my way to heaven with good deeds. I love you and want to be with you. Thank you for everything.

At midnight, Hannah clutched a small suitcase and snuck out of her house. Tears streaming down her face, she rushed into her new life with Peter and with Christ.

Life Application

Salvation can never be earned by obeying a set of rules. It is a gift, purchased through Jesus Christ's death, burial, and resurrection. God freely offers eternal life to all those who come to Him in childlike faith and repent of their sin. Titus 3:5 (KJV) tells us, "Not by works of righteousness which we have done, but according to his mercy he saved us." Praise the Lord for His boundless gift of love!

About the Author

Marsha Hubler, author of the best-selling Keystone Stables series from Zonderkidz, has twenty books and dozens of short stories and articles in print. She has a master's degree in education and over forty years' experience with children of all ages. She presently works with homeschoolers in her home office. Martha lives in central Pennsylvania with her husband and two dogs.

11

Multiplying Love

by Kelly Wilson Mize

Lily sighed as she watched the clock on the wall count down the minutes until the bell rang. Unlike every other kid in her second-grade class, Lily was not at all excited about the upcoming weekend. *I wonder if I could hide in the bathroom till Monday.* If she were a little more brave, she would try it.

In Lily's world, weekends meant two days of loneliness, hunger, and neglect. At school, she could hang out with her friends, play games, and eat a tasty meal at lunchtime. She felt much happier here than she did at home, or anywhere else, for that matter.

The clock showed ten minutes till three. Lily wondered if her mom had made it to the food bank today. *Maybe she got some peanut butter.* Peanut butter was Lily's absolute favorite food.

"Girls and boys." Mrs. Turner's voice jarred Lily back to the classroom. "Our Valentine's Day party will be next Friday. I've e-mailed a class list to your parents, but I'm also giving you a printed copy for your folders, so please make sure your parents get it."

Good thing. Lily's mom didn't have a computer.

"You should bring one valentine for each of your classmates."

The other students talked excitedly about the party, but Lily's heart sank. She wished she had normal parents, the kind who took their kids to the park on Saturdays, or went out to dinner sometimes, or could afford to buy valentines.

The simple cards weren't very expensive. And Valentine's Day only came once a year. But her mother never remembered to get them. Lily would buy them herself if she had the money. She considered sneaking a few dollars from her mom's purse. But she'd be in deep trouble if she got caught. A small box of valentines would probably fit in her backpack. But she didn't feel right about stealing.

Maybe she'd just stay home from school the day of the party.

In kindergarten, when Lily arrived at school on Valentine's Day with nothing to share with her classmates, her teacher had told her it didn't matter. "Don't worry, sweetie. Everyone has plenty of valentines. They won't even notice."

But what her classmates soon forgot stayed in Lily's heart.

In first grade, she had tried to make Valentines from scrap paper and crayons she'd collected from the school's waste baskets. But her best efforts had only resulted in crooked hearts and misspelled words. Some of her young friends said nice things, but others made comments like "What's this supposed to be?" and "Why didn't you bring real valentines?" Lily would never try *that* again.

On Wednesday, as Lily unzipped her tattered backpack at the end of the school day, she found a small, colorful box of brand-new valentines. They were the most beautiful cards she'd ever seen, with glittery puppies and kittens declaring heartfelt affection. Lily blinked and stared at them.

Under the box was an envelope with her name written on it. She placed it carefully between the pages of her math book, to read later when she was alone.

When Lily got home, she hid in her room to avoid the watchful eyes of her mother and little brother, then pulled out the envelope. Inside was a sheet of pink paper with red hearts along the edges. The handwriting on it looked a lot like her teacher's. It said, "We love because he first loved us (1 John 4:19). Happy Valentine's Day, Lily. Jesus loves you!"

Lily had gone to church a few times, when a big bus picked up kids in her neighborhood who wanted to go. She remembered singing a fun song there called "Jesus Loves Me."

The teachers at her school didn't talk much about God. But Lily had once heard Mrs. Turner tell another teacher, "I'll pray for you." And she'd seen her reading a Bible a few times when the class returned early from PE.

On Friday morning, during announcements, Lily thought she saw Mrs. Turner give her a special smile, but she couldn't be sure. When the time came to exchange valentines, Lily bounced from her desk. As her friends ripped open the cards she gave them, their smiling responses were the best reward Lily could imagine.

She saved the all-important teacher's valentine for last. Inside, Lily had written a special message: "I love you because you first loved me." When Mrs. Turner read it, she gave Lily a misty-eyed wink.

After the party, Lily's backpack had two remaining unopened valentines: one for her mother and one for her brother. As she watched the clock on the wall count down the minutes until the weekend, Lily actually looked forward to the two-day break from school.

Life Application

Wherever seeds of love are planted, life-changing growth is possible. When a simple act of love is shared with another person, the results may not be seen or understood immediately (or ever this side of heaven), but love always makes a difference. Because "whoever pursues righteousness and love finds life, prosperity and honor" (Proverbs 21:21).

God loves us so much that He sent His only Son to die so that our sins would be forgiven. There's no greater love than that!

What can you do today to show love to those around you? No act of love is too small, because when it is shared, love multiplies!

About the Author

Kelly Wilson Mize is a wife, mother, educator, and freelance writer living in Huntsville, Alabama. Her work has appeared in a variety of publications for children and adults. Her credits include stories, articles, devotions, and curriculum for LifeWay Christian Resources, Group Publishing, Adams Media, and Focus on the Family. Kelly recently became a copyeditor with the Christian Editor Connection and a member of The Christian PEN. She has a master's degree in elementary education and serves as a librarian at Westminster Christian Academy.

12

A Time to Remember

by Terrie Todd

Judy's eyes opened wide at the ruckus. She squinted in the brightness of the overhead light and looked at the clock. Three ten in the morning. Her husband of two years rummaged through the closet, banging drawers and filling suitcases. Again.

"Bob, what are you doing?"

"I'm leaving."

Judy sighed and swung her feet to the floor, grabbing her robe from the foot of the bed. Last week, he'd managed to fill his car with his belongings while she was at work—and nearly succeeded in driving away. Three nights earlier, he'd done just as he was doing tonight.

"Bob. Look at me." She tilted his chin toward her and waited. Eventually he made eye contact. "You can't go anywhere right now. It's the middle of the night. Do you understand?"

"I'm leaving. You can't stop me." He tossed a lone sock on top of the stack and began zipping the suitcase.

"Where are you going?"

"Home."

"You are home, sweetheart. Why don't you lie down and go back to sleep?"

He stared at her. Slowly, a tear made its way down a wrinkle in his cheek.

"C'mon." Judy pried the suitcase from his hand. "If you still want to leave in the morning, I'll help you. But right now we both need to sleep. Let me get you back to bed."

She felt relieved when he allowed her to tuck him in. She hid the suitcase in the back of the closet, turned off the light, and padded to the kitchen for a drink of water.

Wiping a tear from her cheek, she walked to the computer. She opened the dementia log that Dr. Thompson had recommended she keep. She recorded this new episode beside the date and time. In the right column, reserved for journaling her feelings, she wrote:

I'm so frustrated. I don't know how much longer I can keep this up. Is it time to tell the City they need to start looking for a new water clerk? I can't afford to retire. Besides, Dr. Thompson says it's good for me to get out of the house, as long as Bob can still function on his own. But what if he leaves a burner on or the doors wide open?

God, if it's okay to be completely honest with You, I have to admit … I am bitterly disappointed with my life right now. I could really use Your help.

She closed the laptop, rested her elbows on the desk, and rubbed her eyes with the heels of her hands. Single until the age of fifty-five, Judy had endured years of match-ups with Mister Wrongs by well-meaning friends. She'd given up on the idea of romance long ago and contented herself with her career, her friends, and her faith. She ushered at church, played golf in the summer, and bowled in the winter.

It was through the bowling league that Judy was introduced to the handsome widower, ten years her senior. Bob left his own church to attend Judy's, and it thrilled her heart to hear his rich tenor as he worshipped the Lord beside her. In no time, he became a highly valued member of the choir. When he picked her up for bowling nights, his rendition of "Hey, Jude" melted her heart.

Bob's three grown children supported their blossoming romance. They carried out Bob and Judy's wedding plans and helped them move into their new condo. Judy became an instant grandmother to Bryce's five-year-old twins. She could hardly believe God had brought love and family into her life at this stage.

Now the words of her wedding vows throbbed in her head. "For better, for worse. For richer, for poorer. In sickness and in health …"

Who could have guessed that six months after the honeymoon her husband would begin to display signs of dementia? Their second anniversary had come and gone with Bob mostly unaware.

She turned off the kitchen light, climbed the stairs, and

crawled back into bed. Ninety minutes before the alarm clock was set to go off.

At her office, Judy sifted through a stack of unreasonably high water bills. When she came across her own, her heart sank. Bob had taken to doing laundry while she was at work, and she often returned home to discover one lone item still damp in the washer or a sweater shrunken in the dryer. How many "loads" was he doing? How long could she afford to let this go on?

When she arrived home late that afternoon, Bob was singing a lively rendition of "How Firm a Foundation" as he stirred spaghetti sauce in a pot on the stove. She set the table, relieved to find him lucid.

"We should go bowling tonight," he suggested.

Her first inclination was to complain of tiredness. But how many more opportunities would the two of them have to do fun activities together? "Sounds like a fine idea."

After an enjoyable dinner, complete with small talk, Bob cleared the table while Judy filled the sink with hot, soapy water.

"You're not Karen," Bob said, standing in the middle of the kitchen, dirty plate in hand.

She took a deep breath. "No, I'm Judy. Your new wife."

He stared at her a moment. "Where's Karen?"

"Karen died. Remember?"

He continued to stare, and the focused expression on his face told her he was working hard. "Oh, yeah," he said slowly.

Judy took the plate and Bob sat, gripping the edge of the

table. "I can't believe she's gone." Fresh tears trickled down his face and dripped onto his shirt.

How many times would he have to relive his grief … and break Judy's heart in the process?

A knock at the door interrupted them. Bryce stuck his head in the door. "You guys home?"

"Come on in." Judy felt the instant relief that came with the presence of another adult whenever Bob was like this. "Your dad and I were thinking of going bowling tonight."

"Good for you." He moved close to Judy. "You look a little tired. Rough day?"

She nodded.

Bryce clapped a hand on his father's shoulder. "Hey, Dad, want to bowl with me tonight?"

Bob looked up at his son. "Thanks, Tim. I'd like that."

Bryce didn't bother to correct his father. It didn't really matter whether Bob recognized which of his sons he bowled with. He'd be happy either way. And Judy could enjoy a nice break, knowing he was in good hands.

Bryce handed Bob his jacket from the hook and opened the back door. "See you in a couple of hours, Judy. Try to get some rest."

"Thank you," she mouthed.

"No problem."

When they were gone, Judy collapsed on the sofa. She opened her Bible and let it land somewhere near the middle. The words of Isaiah 41:10 were highlighted in bright yellow: "Do not fear, for I am with you; do not be dismayed, for I am your God. I will strengthen you and help you; I will uphold you with my righteous right hand."

Judy read the verse over and over until she cried herself to sleep.

She awoke refreshed and ready to care for her husband again. When the men returned, Bob acted perfectly normal … and remained that way for the next two days.

Needing a break from staring at numbers for hours on end, Judy entered the break room. She headed for the tray of bagels on the counter. As she poured hot water into a cup, three coworkers came in, discussing a news story about a young couple who'd gotten into a car accident on their wedding night.

"The groom just has a couple of broken ribs," Susan said, "but the bride is paralyzed for life."

"I wonder how long *their* marriage will last." Rebecca shook her head. "He sure didn't sign up for that!"

"Actually," Judy said, "he did." She stirred sugar into her tea. "If he truly meant his wedding vows, he signed up for better or for worse. In sickness and in health. Maybe the reason they're together is not so much for his happiness, but because God knew she would need him."

The women stared at the floor. They all knew about Judy's situation and sympathized. But they couldn't truly relate to her struggles.

Judy's own words continued to penetrate her heart as she carried on with her workday.

She and Bob didn't have a long history together. But she wasn't alone. His kids would do all they could for both of them, and they'd be there when the time came for tough decisions.

More important, God hadn't abandoned her. He would always be her help and her strength.

Life Application

Disappointment with God can weigh us down, and the unfairness of our circumstances often robs us of joy and causes us to question His goodness and His plan. In those times we need to press into the truth of His Word. He will not leave you. He will never abandon you. He loves you.

If you are a caregiver, God will grant you the strength to remain faithful to the task. Indeed, He is the only one who can. During the tough times in life, Scripture verses like Lamentations 3:22–24 become more real to us than ever before: "Because of the LORD's great love we are not consumed, for his compassions never fail. They are new every morning; great is your faithfulness. I say to myself, 'The LORD is my portion; therefore I will wait for him.'"

About the Author

Terrie Todd has published several Chicken Soup for the Soul stories and two full-length plays. She writes a weekly Faith and Humor column for the *Central Plains Herald Leader*, and her first novel, *The Silver Suitcase*, was released by Waterfall Press in January 2016. She lives in Manitoba, Canada, with her husband, Jon, and works as an administrative assistant at City Hall. Find her at terrietodd.blogspot.com.

13

On the Mountaintop

by Nanette Thorsen-Snipes

Gabrielle stood in the kitchen of her rustic cabin, watching an orange sun melt along the mountaintops in North Georgia, draping them in a curtain of pale yellow. Her daughter, Bethany, would turn sixteen on Valentine's Day—only three days away. Where had the years gone?

Valentine's Day had always held a special place in Gabby's heart. Jake had proposed to her on February 14, and they'd chosen that day to get married. They celebrated their anniversaries taking weekend trips to exotic places. Every year he brought along a gift basket filled with chocolates, bath salts, a music CD, and scented candles. On one romantic getaway, they had decided to start a family. A year later, their sweet baby girl was born—by romantic coincidence, on Valentine's Day.

Gabby placed her hand over her pounding heart. Memories tumbled like the waterfalls she and Jake had visited, and so did her tears. Two years ago, they'd enjoyed an intimate dinner on the outdoor patio of a quaint bungalow, wrapped up in their winter garb. It had been so romantic, so perfect.

Until he told her he had cancer.

Soon after her husband's death, Gabby lost her well-paying job due to the economic downturn. She'd made less money with each new position. She now worked hard at being the best cook and maid at a little bed-and-breakfast. She assisted the owners in the kitchen by preparing meals, cleaning rooms, making beds, and making sure customers were content.

Their little cabin on the property was meager but sufficient. In the back of her mind, Gabby wondered how her once-perfect life had gone so wrong.

She also wondered where God was when she needed Him. Her fundamentalist background rose up to mock her. God is good. He is awesome. He will provide. But how could she trust a God who allowed her childhood to be rife with abuse, and who took from her the only man she'd ever loved?

"Mom!" Her daughter's insistent voice pierced her thoughts.

"In here."

Bethany barged in, combing through her sun-streaked hair with long, slender fingers. "So, what are we going to do for my birthday?"

Gabby's heart sank. "We're broke, Bethany!" The words tumbled out before she thought.

Her daughter's shoulders slumped. "Angie got a new car for her birthday. And Jamie's getting an iPhone."

Gabby choked on the tears she tried to keep at bay. "I—I'm sorry, honey."

Bethany's usually sparkling green eyes dimmed. "I thought you had some insurance money left."

"I had to pay off the rest of the medical bills. Honey, I'm doing the best I can."

Even as Jake was lying in that sterile hospital room, a morphine drip barely keeping the pain tolerable, he repeatedly said, "I can do all things through Christ who strengthens me," quoting Philippians 4:13 (NKJV). If her husband could smile through his catastrophic ordeal, why did she struggle so much with simple, day-to-day trials?

Her daughter's lower lip plumped up. "But it's my sixteenth, Mom."

"I'll figure out something, sweetie. You'll have the best birthday I'm able to give."

With an exaggerated sigh, Bethany fled the room.

After cleaning ten rooms and making beds, Gabby sat in front of the fireplace in the empty lobby, warming her hands. How would she give her only child a special gift on her milestone birthday? *Lord, I am at my wit's end. But I trust You. Like Jake used to say, I can do all things through Christ. Please help me.*

As she stretched her hands closer to the fire, the small diamonds in her wedding ring sparkled and danced in the firelight. The ring had been Jake's grandmother's, then his mother's, and now it belonged to her. In a flash of inspiration, she knew what she needed to do.

Gabby drove to a jewelry store that afternoon and had the ring cleaned. Then she went to the drug store and bought wrapping paper, a small box, and three birthday cards.

February 14 arrived with a flurry of light snow. Gabby was relieved that the day fell in the middle of the week, so there wouldn't be much work to do. When Bethany crawled out of bed and joined her in the kitchen before school, Gabby was ready.

"Happy birthday, sweetheart." On the round oak table lay three envelopes and a small box wrapped in blue foil.

Bethany tilted her head, her sunlit brown hair draping over her slim shoulders. "What's that?"

"Your birthday present." Gabby took a sip of tea, then poured her daughter a cup, adding a touch of stevia and some milk. Bethany drank some, then put the mug down and picked up the box.

"You have to open the cards first."

She raised an eyebrow as she read the first card out loud. "Have a happy birthday, Bethany. I wish I could have known you, but I know God does, and He will always care for you. Hope you enjoy the gift! Love, Great-Grandmother Irma."

Bethany bit her lower lip to keep from choking up. "Mom . . . that's your handwriting."

"I know." Gabby pushed the second card toward her daughter. "Open this one next."

Bethany slowly opened the blue envelope and read the note inside. "I wish I had been around to see you grow up and become a beautiful young lady. I know we would have been good friends. I love you, Bethany. Love, Grandmother Enid."

Tears pooled in Bethany's eyes as she opened the last envelope. "Bethany, I want you to have my gift of love on your special day. This gift is from all of us, including your dad. You are so loved—by us and by God. Mom."

With slow determination, Bethany removed the bow from the top of the package and carefully unwrapped the small box. Inside was the diamond ring her father's great-grandmother, grandmother, and mother had owned and cherished.

Bethany held it up to the light and it sparkled brilliantly. She slipped it onto the ring finger of her right hand. "It fits! Mom, this is the best birthday present anyone could ever have!" She reached across the table and hugged her mother tightly.

Gabby glanced out at the sun's rays glistening on snow-covered branches. She silently thanked God for providing a gift where there was no gift—a ring with a legacy of love from three godly women.

Life Application

Have you been through tough times? Is it impossible to see a way out? Trusting in our human strength to survive trials seems natural. But when we come up against a brick wall of circumstances beyond our control, we come to the realization that, in our human frailty, there is no hope. But God will make a way where there is no way if we trust in Him. Philippians 4:13 says, "I can do all this through him who gives me strength." When you trust in God, you conquer the valleys and rise to the top of the mountain.

About the Author

Nanette Thorsen-Snipes has published more than five hundred articles, columns, and reprints in more than forty publications and fifty-nine compilation books, including stories in three Guideposts anthologies in the Miracles series, in *The New Women's Devotional Bible*, and in *Grace Givers*. She lives in North Georgia with her husband, Jim. They have four grown children and eight grandchildren. Find her at FaithWorksEditorial.com.

14

Call It

by Rachael Landis

We're over," I said, gazing into Dereck's cavern-blue eyes across the table at our favorite Seattle downtown café.

"What do you mean?"

"I can't do this anymore."

"Do what?" His eyebrows crunched together. "Be friends with me?"

I nodded, hoping my silent reply would vanish into the spinning air around us.

We'd met at university, two lonely freshmen finding a comfortable kinship with each other. I had never dated nor had any desire to. Burned by a childhood sweetheart, he only wanted friendship. A perfect match. Over the years, we remained close friends.

Lately, we'd grown too close for comfort. My comfort, anyway.

I watched pedestrians and cars moving outside the window. Anything to avoid looking into Dereck's intense gaze. "We've been friends forever. But we're so much more. You bring me soup when I'm sick and flowers when I'm sad. I pick out your tie for meetings. We've never seen an episode of *America's Got Talent* except together."

His mouth opened, but I rushed on.

"No guys will date me because of my relationship with you. And you know Karen doesn't like me." His girlfriend of six months never said she hated me, but I saw it in her eyes and heard it in her voice.

"Karen likes you," he protested weakly.

I resisted the urge to take his hand. "Dereck, I love being your friend. But we've gone beyond friendship. We need to make our relationship official or end it." I regretted my words the moment they left my lips. I turned away so he couldn't see the hope in my eyes.

"Can't we just stay the way we are?" he pleaded, like a child begging for another piece of chocolate cake.

"The cost of our friendship is too high. We need to call it, one way or the other." Under the table, I crossed my fingers. *Please pick the first option.* My pulse pounded in my temples.

He stared at me, speechless.

"This was a mistake. I need to go." I dug through my purse and plunked money onto the table. I didn't look back until I reached the café door. Unable to resist the pull, I turned around. Dereck looked tired and old, like my father the day we got the news of my grandfather's death.

I almost rushed back to offer a white flag. Instead I marched out.

I spent close to an hour wandering the city's streets, avoiding going back to my apartment. I didn't want to face all the pictures of us there. Our college group trip to the Rocky Mountains. Goofing off at Disneyland. Getting sunburned at the beach.

When the evening sunlight faded, I trudged home to a lonely, cold apartment. I went straight to bed, ignoring the pictures decorating my walls and sitting on my furniture.

Dereck didn't call the next day. Or the day after that. *He's probably just busy with work,* I told myself. But I grieved the loss of the most important person in my life.

My coworkers didn't say anything about my morose attitude, as if they were afraid a terrible storm would be released if they prodded me. But I saw their suspicious glances and heard their whispers about why I regularly came to work early and left late. The only company I kept was my computer and the health-tips book I was editing for the publishing house I worked for.

My prayers echoed in my living room like a moaning wind through an abandoned ship. My thoughts transformed into an ocean of crashing waves. *He doesn't want me.*

On the ninth day after presenting my pushy ultimatum, when I arrived home from work, I found a letter on the floor. I dropped my purse and tore open the envelope.

Dereck's sprawling handwriting broke through my fog.

Lucy,

You're right. I think it's time we call it.

Meet me at the metro station at 7 tonight. I'll wait if I need to.

Dereck

I closed my eyes and bit my lip. This could go either way. But I couldn't stop a bubble of excitement from rippling through my stomach.

I stumbled down my apartment's stairs, dodging my neighbors and ignoring the guy who hollered, "Hey, lady, watch where you're going!"

Outside, the Seattle rain choked the sun, and fog drifted over the pedestrians going from home to work or back. We moved in unison, our steps pounding the streets in a rhythmic dance.

I finally arrived at the top of the metro station. Breathless, I stopped and rested against the rail, trying to prepare myself for whatever Dereck had to say. After counting to three, I took a deep breath, then rushed down the stairs.

Dozens of eyes met mine at the platform. Navy-blue coats, bright-yellow umbrellas, and peachy scarves created a rainbow of hues in the dreary station.

"Lucy!"

My head swiveled in the direction of that familiar voice.

Dereck stood there, amid the colors, dressed in a green polo and blue jeans. In his hands he held a white poster board. In bold red letters, it declared, "I chose option one."

Stares and whispers surrounded me, along with a few phones held up to capture this odd moment. I stripped the distance between us in seconds.

With arched eyebrows and folded arms, I asked, "What about Karen?"

"We broke up."

"Because of me?"

Dereck's grin brought out a dimple. "Actually, she got a work promotion that entailed the possibility of moving. So we decided to stop seeing each other."

My trembling hands clasped his. "So I guess we can continue being friends?"

"Forever friends." His fingertips caressed my cheek. "And so much more."

Life Application

One of my favorite books is *Love Comes Softly* by Janette Oke, a story about two strangers on the American frontier pushed into marriage by circumstances. Their friendship grows out of necessity, but by the end, they have learned to love each other.

Hollywood has inundated us with movies about grand love stories about love at first sight and the fireworks that come along with it. But true love is often discovered though the ordinary parts of life.

Friendship is a valuable gift. God created human beings to be in relationship with Him and others. In Ecclesiastes 4:9–10, King Solomon says, "Two are better than one, because they have a good return for their work: If either of them falls down, one can help the other up. But pity anyone who falls and has no one to help them up!"

About the Author

Rachael Landis grew up on the sunny Caribbean islands of Barbados and Jamaica as a missionary kid. She is now pursuing an associate of arts degree for professional writing while working as a nanny and a caregiver for the elderly. Her favorite things are cats, chocolate, cake, and chocolate cake! Of course, she also likes reading.

15

Love Deeply

by Sherry Kyle

I sliced carrots and potatoes and put them in the pot to boil. Matthew loved my chicken pot pie. And I wanted to show my husband that I loved him this Valentine's Day, despite our strained marriage.

Matthew and I had handpicked everything in our newly remodeled kitchen, down to the hardware and pendant lighting. No interior designer was needed. We'd scoured the Internet, looking for do-it-yourself projects to save money … and our relationship.

But that was a year ago. A year filled with deep hurts. Lack of communication, punctuated by harsh words. Destruction of our faith, in God and in each other.

I set a large skillet on the left burner and heated a cup of butter along with chopped onion. As I stirred in flour and seasonings, chicken broth, and milk, I wondered why I even bothered preparing a romantic candlelit dinner when Matthew and I were barely speaking.

Was it too late for us?

Blinking back tears, I added the chicken, peas, cooked carrots and potatoes, then turned down the heat. I unrolled a pastry sheet into a nine-inch pie plate, trimming off the extra dough before adding the chicken mixture and covering the top with another pastry sheet. After cutting a few slits on the top to let air escape, I sealed and fluted the edges.

If only we could go back in time, back to when I was pregnant. Before the miscarriage. When we actually spent time together instead of living like roommates. Back when we were nurturing our marriage and fulfilling our vows to love, honor, and cherish each other the way Christ loved the church. That felt like such a long time ago.

The doorbell rang. I wiped my hands on the nearest towel and hurried to the door.

My longtime friend Amanda stood on the porch with a big smile. "Come with me for a pedicure."

I glanced at the clock. The pot pie only needed a half hour in the oven. Matthew had been working late almost every night, coming home after I'd eaten and watched a television show or two. It was his turn to wait on me.

"Give me a minute to turn off the oven and stick dinner in the refrigerator." I headed for the kitchen.

"Oh, and grab your pink nail polish. You always say Matthew loves that color on you."

As if painted toenails would improve my marriage.

Fifteen minutes later Amanda and I sat in adjacent chairs at the nail salon, our feet in hot, bubbly water.

Amanda chose a French pedicure—crisp and clean, like so many things in her life. She and her husband, Joshua, had a perfectly furnished two-story house, complete with white picket fence and four adorable children.

"So who's watching the kids?" I asked, putting on a brave face.

"Josh came home early from work so I could sneak out for a little while."

I tamped down my jealous thoughts and closed my eyes, concentrating on the woman's hands rubbing my feet and calves. I didn't want to be envious of my best friend. But my evening would be lonely with no children to fill the void.

As our nails dried, my mother-in-law walked in. What was she doing here? "Heather, I'm glad I caught you. Macy's is having a sale, and I found the perfect dress for you."

I glanced at Amanda, and she shrugged.

"Go try it on," my friend said. "Text me a picture and show me how it looks."

"I can drive you to the mall and take you home after," Linda said.

"Are you sure you don't mind?" Ever since Matthew's parents bought a house in the senior community across town, heavy traffic prevented us from visiting during the week.

"It's no problem at all. It'll be nice to catch up."

I hugged Amanda good-bye and followed my mother-in-law to the parking lot. As I slid into her sedan, I noticed a few shopping bags in the backseat.

A short ride later, we walked up to the check-out counter at Macy's, where the cashier had the dress on hold. Surprisingly, it was the same shade of pink that covered my freshly polished toenails.

Linda held up the dress and twirled it around, the chiffon material dancing with her movement. "Do you like it?"

Like it? I loved it.

The bodice appeared fitted, with a swath of sheer pink fabric crossing over one shoulder, the hem hitting a couple of inches above the knee. The dress was a classic design, and I hoped it looked as good on me as it did on the hanger.

I grinned. "I'd love to try it on."

"I'll wait out here." Linda leaned against the wall adjacent to the fitting room. "Call me if you need help with the zipper. If it doesn't fit, let me know and I'll bring you a different size."

I glanced at the price tag and swallowed hard. There was no way I could buy this dress without conferring with Matthew. We'd decided long ago to talk about items that cost more than a hundred dollars before we purchased them. The last thing I wanted was another argument.

Linda winked. "Consider it a gift."

"Oh, I couldn't—"

She touched my hand. "I know you and Matthew have had a rough time lately, and you deserve something special."

I couldn't force myself to turn down her generous offer.

The dress *was* fabulous. Fortunately, I fit into a smaller size than the one Linda had picked for me.

After the dress was purchased and wrapped, my mother-in-law hooked her hand in the crook of my arm and suggested we look for strappy sandals to go with it. And while we were at it, I should get a makeover too.

As I walked to Linda's sedan wearing the new dress and shoes, with my make-up professionally done, guilt nagged at me. How much did my mother-in-law know about my marriage? If she had any idea how bad things really were, she might not have spent all that money on me.

"Thank you so much," I said for the third or fourth time since we exited the mall.

"Don't think anything of it." Linda swatted the air. "You know how much I love to shop."

Once we were settled in the car, Linda drove out of the parking lot. At the freeway entrance, instead of turning toward my house, she headed in the opposite direction.

"I think we're going the wrong way." I cringed. Where was she taking me now?

"I have one more errand to run. I hope you don't mind."

I sank into the seat. "Not at all."

Moments later, she pulled into the parking lot of Le Chateâu restaurant, known for its fine French cuisine. I'd driven by the place a hundred times but had never dared step foot inside.

Linda got out of the car. I followed her in.

The restaurant was everything I'd dreamed it would be, with dark burgundy chairs and a ceiling that beautifully contrasted the buff color of the walls, creating a warm, rustic environment. White tablecloths and vases filled with brightly colored flowers graced the tables.

When I turned to tell Linda how amazing the place looked, I saw Matthew standing where she'd been, dressed in a navy suit and tie, holding a bouquet of pink roses. He was just as handsome as the day I married him, if not more so.

Linda gave me a wink, then slipped out the entrance.

"These are for you," Matthew said, his voice uncertain.

I took the roses, inhaling their beautiful scent. "What's going on?"

"I asked Mom and Amanda to get you ready for tonight. They were more than willing." He shifted his weight. "Did you enjoy your afternoon?"

Had my husband planned the pedicure, the new dress and shoes, the makeover, and now this? My throat constricted.

A verse from Scripture, 1 Peter 4:8, came to mind. "Above all, love each other deeply, because love covers over a multitude of sins." Matthew—and our heavenly Father—had forgiven me for my part in our strained marriage and wiped the slate clean. Now it was my turn to forgive.

Lord, thank You for my husband.

I looked into Matthew's deep-blue eyes, as warm as the ocean. "I loved every minute of my afternoon. And I love you!"

"I love you too." He gave me a tender kiss that promised many more to come.

There were still some serious things we needed to discuss. But there'd be time for that later. After we enjoyed our romantic dinner at Le Chateâu.

Life Application

Relationships take a lot of work. Sometimes we say and do things we regret, and instead of asking for forgiveness and moving on, we push down our hurts and keep them to ourselves, allowing them to build over time. As soon as the next stressful situation pops up, we explode. Our relationships will suffer if we don't take time to nurture them and communicate.

The apostle Paul wrote, in Ephesians 4:2–3, "Be completely humble and gentle; be patient, bearing with one another in love. Make every effort to keep the unity of the Spirit through the bond of peace." If we take these verses to heart, we will live harmoniously with those around us.

But we can't build strong marriages on our own. Ecclesiastes 4:12 says, "Though one may be overpowered, two can defend themselves. A cord of three strands is not quickly broken." Two together can be strong, but with God, we're much stronger. If we invite Him to be the third strand in our marriages, we can weather even the harshest storm.

About the Author

Sherry Kyle is an award-winning author who writes books for tween girls as well as contemporary and historical novels for women. She is a graduate of Biola University and has been married to Douglas, her college sweetheart, for twenty-seven years. They have four almost-grown children and make their home on the California coast. Visit Sherry on the Web at sherrykyle.com.

16

A Finger and a Big Toe

by Nancy Ellen Hird

Though the calendar read Friday, it had been Monday all day. I had to drive carpool. The dog found a skunk … again. My computer crashed, the dishwasher died, the soccer game went into overtime, and now I had to make a cake. I glared at the recipe and back at the egg carton. Two eggs, and the recipe called for three. I flipped to the front of the cookbook. Where was that section on substitutions?

"Mom," Matt's voice called as the front door slammed. "Mom!" His voice grew closer and louder. What now?

Glancing over my shoulder I saw my thirteen-year-old son and behind him my friend Carla. She wore her good navy-blue coat, and her usually tousled blonde hair was Sunday-morning sleek.

"Am I too early, Becky?" she asked.

I wanted to sink into the floor. "Oh, Carla," I groaned, "I forgot about the church play."

She smiled and shrugged. "Don't worry about it. They're doing a performance tomorrow night too. Maybe you could go then. I'll go by myself tonight. It's OK."

I looked at the cake ingredients assembled on the counter. What Carla said made sense. I mean, besides the cake, there was laundry to fold, bills to pay, and people on the fund-raising committee I needed to call.

Carla turned to leave. I felt awful. I was breaking a promise. And I felt an inner urging to do something about it. "Wait," I said. "Give me a minute."

She slid out of her coat. "How can I help?"

We put that cake together in record time. As I threw on my jacket, I threatened Matt that I'd hide his cell phone if he didn't take the cake out when the buzzer sounded. He rolled his eyes but nodded.

Carla and I left for the church. We pulled into the parking lot with moments to spare.

The sanctuary was beautiful, filling me with a much-needed peace. Settling back against the soft cushion of the pew, I sighed. "Thanks so much for—"

I caught my breath when I saw Jennifer Wright coming down the aisle. She and Tracey, one of the new board members of the women's shelter, stopped to talk with someone a few rows back.

I took a sudden interest in the program in my lap. It's amazing how fascinating they can be, given the right circumstances.

I heard Jennifer slip into the pew behind me. I glued my eyes to the program, my stomach churning.

Of all the people in the world, why did she have to be here? This wasn't her church. And why did she have to be here tonight? And sit right behind me?

Stop being childish, I told myself. I glanced back, caught her eye, and nodded. I opened my mouth to speak, but the lights dimmed at that moment so I didn't have to say anything.

Swallowing hard, I stared at the ceiling. Up front a guitar and a flute started a duet, but I barely heard them.

Ever since I began volunteering for the women's shelter, I wanted Jennifer to like me. I admired her so much. I tried to be her friend. I invited her to lunch. To coffee. But she never accepted. I prayed about our relationship. I prayed about it daily for a while. Finally I admitted that I had failed. She didn't want anything more than a surface relationship with me.

I shifted uneasily against the pew. Would tonight open up all those wounds? God, why did she have to be here? Why didn't I just stay home and bake that cake?

I tried concentrating on the play. It portrayed a woman's walk with the Lord: the conflicts, disappointments, failures, triumphs. I identified with everything but the triumphs.

When the play ended, I knew I was going to have to speak to Jennifer. *Just do it*, I told myself. I turned around, hoping I was too late and that she'd already left. But she hadn't. I pasted on my best smile. "Hi, Jen, how's it going?"

"Oh, not too bad. Though I'm starting to wish I'd never bought all that crystal and china. I love every piece, but it's such a chore to wrap them up. The movers will do some—"

"You're moving?" I cut in.

"Yes. Peter was transferred to the Denver office. We leave in two weeks."

"Oh." I was dumbfounded.

"It's a great opportunity. But we will miss being here."

"I—I'm sure it'll be a good thing … eventually," I managed to say. "But I can't imagine how the shelter will get along without you."

"Oh, they'll find someone. But that's sweet of you to say."

If I asked her to lunch, what would she say?

"I've enjoyed working with you." Jennifer smiled.

"Thanks. It's been a pleasure for me too."

She and Tracey inched their way out of the pew. The conversation was over. Along with my hopes for our friendship. "Take care," I muttered.

I caught Carla's glances of concern as we headed for the parking lot. "Are you all right?" she asked when we got into her car.

"Yeah. I just hoped things could work out between Jennifer and me. I guess it wasn't meant to be. She never liked me."

Carla shook her head. "She liked you. You told me she often asked for your advice, was always seeing if you could head up this committee or that. It sounds to me like she admired you a lot." Carla sent me a quick glance. "She just didn't want to be your best friend," she said tenderly.

The comment cut close to the bone. And I knew it was true. I had wanted Jennifer to be my best friend, though I had never put it into those words. I'd assumed that when I asked God to work out the relationship, being best friends was the only acceptable answer.

As Carla drove, an even more startling revelation occurred to me. Could God have said no for a reason? If Jennifer and I had become best friends, would it have cost me something that God didn't want me to pay? Would the relationship have been wrong for me? Or for her?

"But Christians are supposed to be close," I said. "I mean, we're the body of Christ."

"That's right." Carla grinned impishly. "But …"

"But what?" I frowned.

"Well, what if you're a finger and she's a big toe? The body would end up with an awful aching back if you two were really close."

I broke out laughing. "Oh, Carla, you're such a hoot!"

She laughed too. "Coffee at your house?"

"Great idea!" I smiled all the way from my head down to my big toe … and thanked God for giving me a friend like Carla.

Life Application

Growing up, I had a few good friends, but I felt worried or frustrated when I couldn't develop closer friendships with the people I admired most. After I became a Christian in my twenties, I assumed that my "failed" relationships were the result of sin. I'd been a bad person, or the other person was a sinner, or we were both so bad we could never be buddies.

But one day my pastor said that godly people could have different levels of relationships. He described four types.

Intimate friendships are the most intense and involve a high degree of trust. Close friendships are less intense, but people still choose to be together, often because they share a common interest or goal. Casual relationships are found in work or classroom settings where people can't choose who they are with. Acquaintances are people we meet regularly in our community; we know little about them and they know little about us.

Seeing relationships in that way brought me great relief. I no longer felt baffled or insulted when people who seemingly appreciated me didn't invite me to dinner at their house. I stopped feeling guilty about not sharing the intimate details of my life with people I hardly knew.

As I studied the Bible, I saw that Jesus, during His public ministry, had different degrees of intimacy with His followers. Peter, James, and John witnessed the raising of Jairus's daughter, the transfiguration, and the agony of Jesus in Gethsemane, events the other disciples and most of His followers did not see. Jesus didn't invite many to be part of those moments. He loved every person He encountered, but He did not relate to all of them in the same way.

Intimate friendships require huge time and energy commitments. They are also very influential. Human beings are only capable of having a few intimate friends at a time. We need not fret when a close friendship or a casual relationship does not deepen. We can entrust every relationship to God.

About the Author

Nancy Ellen Hird likes to write in a variety of genres. She is the author of *I Get a Clue—from My Edinburgh Files*, a mystery novel for girls ages ten to thirteen. To learn more about this novel, visit desertfirespress.com. Nancy has also written numerous articles and is a contributor to *Chicken Soup for the Christian Woman's Soul, The Heart of a Teacher,* and *The Embrace of a Father*. She is a passionate advocate for children and has reviewed children's literature for Focus on the Family.

17

The Candy Bowl

by Christine Henderson

Maggie cut open the bag of pink and red M&Ms and poured them into the opalescent Carnival-glass candy dish on her office desk. How many times had her fingers slipped into that bowl as a child to retrieve similar candies on Valentine's Day? Back then, the bowl sat on the coffee table in her grandparents' living room and was always full of seasonal sweets when she came to visit after school.

She popped a couple of candies in her mouth and then placed a note beside the bowl, just like her grandmother used to do. The note read, "Tell me about your day."

She ran her finger around the rim of the bowl and smiled. *Thanks, Grams, for sending me a little bit of home.*

She sat in front of her computer and reviewed her office e-mail. Soon she was absorbed in writing and reviewing reports.

Two hours later, her coworker Stephanie knocked on her open door. "Got a minute?"

Maggie waved her in and leaned back in her chair.

"I have new numbers for Kayson Homes that I'd like to discuss with you." Stephanie sat, handed two papers to Maggie, and pointed to the bowl. "Valentine's M&Ms. My favorite. May I have some?"

Maggie pointed to the note beside the bowl. "First you have to tell me about your day."

"Are you serious?"

She nodded. "Family tradition."

"Okay. Well, my day is busy. Lots to do, just like always. But I'll get it all done."

Maggie chuckled. "When I gave that kind of answer to my Grams, she'd say, 'That doesn't cut it.' She wouldn't accept a pat answer. No candy until I opened up about how I was *really* doing."

Stephanie crossed her arms and raised an eyebrow. "And that's what I have to do in order to get a candy?"

"Yep." Maggie leaned forward on her desk and looked Stephanie in the eye. "So, tell me something about your family."

"All right." Stephanie eyed the bowl. "I have two wonderful children. My son, Trent, is in kindergarten and loves bugs. Laura's in third grade and adores stuffed animals. My husband, Logan, is in the army. He's currently deployed, so for now I'm both Mom and Dad."

Maggie pushed the bowl closer to Stephanie. "That must be hard for you."

She took a handful of candies. "It's definitely a challenge being a part-time single parent. But I support my husband and his mission."

As she listened to Stephanie talk, Maggie realized that her interaction with her coworkers consisted mostly of hellos as she passed them in the hall. She'd seen family pictures on Stephanie's desk as she walked by her office, but never asked for any details.

"What about you?" Stephanie asked. "Is there someone special in your life?"

Maggie knew that putting the sign and candy bowl out would mean she'd be asked to reveal personal things about herself. She twisted the band around her left ring finger. After the divorce, she couldn't bear to feel the absence of a wedding band on that finger and replaced it with one that had an assortment of tiny colored gems. It was her way of hiding from the feeling of failure it brought.

She looked up. "Nope. No kids, no husband. Not even a boyfriend."

Stephanie moved the candy bowl toward Maggie. "Sounds like there used to be somebody. What happened?"

She took several M&Ms and rolled them around in the palm of her hand like dice. "I'm divorced. He fell in love with someone else."

"Oh, Maggie, I'm so sorry."

She popped a couple of candies into her mouth. "Our marriage didn't even make it into our second year. The divorce was finalized eight months ago." Maggie hadn't mentioned the breakup to anyone outside of her family and close friends back in her hometown. It felt good to open up to someone she'd see again tomorrow.

"I'd be devastated if Logan ever left me." Stephanie munched on a couple more M&Ms. "How do you handle it?"

Maggie blew out a deep breath. "Depends. Sometimes, like on Valentine's Day, it really hurts. But I have to move on. That's why I took this job. I needed a new location and different people. "

Stephanie slapped her hand on the desk. "Well, I'm going to help you start fresh. On Saturday mornings, I get together with some other moms, and we go out to brunch, without our kids. You've got to come along."

"I'd like that." Maggie felt a lightness in her chest that hadn't been there in a while. She recognized it as hope.

Once they'd made the arrangements of where and when to meet, Stephanie went back to her office and the two women resumed their work.

When Maggie returned to her apartment that evening, she kicked off her shoes, sat cross-legged on the couch, and called her grandmother. Her words bubbled out almost before Grams said hello. "I took your advice and brought your candy bowl to work."

"Good. So, tell me about your day."

"Well, the sign got a coworker to talk to me. I opened up to her too."

"That sounds like a great way to make friends."

Maggie wiped a tear from the corner of her eye. "Thanks for all the times you sat with me and listened to my fears, joys, and uncertainties. Back then, I thought it was only about the chocolate. Now I see it was about caring. How did you get so smart?"

"I learned everything I know about life from the Bible. The book of Hebrews and several of Paul's epistles talk about the importance of encouraging one another. That's what I did for you … and what I hope you'll do for the people God brings into your life."

"I'll do my best."

"I'm sure God will honor that."

Life Application

All the tech gadgets we have today are supposed to help us feel more connected, but they tend to do the opposite. A rapid volley of back-and-forth text messages may be a great way to put your thoughts out there, but it doesn't take the place of someone holding your hand and saying, "I understand."

What a joy it is to grow a treasured relationship that will last a lifetime—with a grandparent, friend, coworker, or—best of all—the Lover of your soul.

About the Author

Christine Henderson enjoys writing in multiple genres. *Berry Blue Haiku* and *Pockets Magazine* have published her children's poems. Her stories about family life have been included in numerous anthologies, most recently in Chicken Soup for the Soul. For the past three years, she's been one of the contributing authors for the quarterly devotional magazine *The Secret Place*. She is an active member of the Christian Writers Group, Romance Writers of America, and Society of Children's Book Writers and Illustrators. Her blog, TheWriteChris.blogspot.com, features weekly interviews with authors and writing tips.

18

Full Pursuit

by Julie DeEtte Williams

A glance in her rearview mirror revealed the flash of red and blue lights. Why did that sight always paralyze Beth—even when she wasn't doing anything wrong?

Step on it, a voice in her head begged. *Lead him on a full pursuit.* Reason proved the stronger friend, and her foot tapped the brake pedal even before her mind registered her speed.

She searched for a pullout … and a reason. No one got stopped on this back road unless they drove more than ten miles an hour over the speed limit. Which she never did. At least not on purpose.

An almond orchard filled with white blossoms welcomed her to the side of the road. Maybe the cruiser would pass her. Surely bigger prey lay ahead.

Nope. He eased in behind her.

Beth pried her fingers from the steering wheel and fumbled the car into park. What had Grandpa told her about how to avoid a ticket? Oh, yeah. Hop out of the car and act innocent. That advice probably didn't work anymore. She placed her hands at two and ten on the steering wheel and held her breath.

The officer slid out of his black-and-white and strolled up to her window, holding his ticket book. Each crunch of his boots on the gravel shoulder echoed through her, buzzing the back of her neck like a dozen angry bees.

He crouched down beside her window, meeting her face-to-face. "License, registration, and proof of insurance, please."

She took her driver's license from her wallet and the paperwork out of the glove box and handed them to him. As he copied down her information, she stared at her reflection in his mirrored sunglasses. An eternity passed as a spring breeze flirted with the little blossoms.

When he returned the cards, she gave him a tentative smile. "Was I speeding, officer?"

He removed his glasses and pocketed them like it was pure reflex. "No, miss."

Something worse than speeding. Cell phone? She'd ignored the last text—scratch one infraction off the list. Passing on the wrong side? She hadn't seen another car in … who knew how long? Tiny spasms rolled through her stomach. Could a girl get ticketed for barfing on a police officer's boots?

Another eternity passed. "Was my driving unsafe?" She honeyed her words to get them past the knot in her throat.

"Oh, no, miss."

"Something wrong with my car?"

"Afraid so." His calm tone bordered on playfulness.

Okay, she'd go along with it. Who didn't love a good mystery? Beth tilted her head, raised an eyebrow, and waited.

"Your right blinker is out."

"Is that why it ticks faster than the left one?"

He nodded and tore a page from his ticket book. "I'm just giving you a fix-it notice." He handed it to her. "After you replace the light, mail your proof of correction to the address on the form."

"Okay."

"One more thing, Miss Adams."

"Yes?"

"May I … call you sometime?" A deep shade of red crept up his sun-browned face. "To, uh, make sure you took care of the violation."

The invisible bees swarmed from her neck to her ears, each with a snarky answer, but none worth repeating. Grandpa never covered this in his how-to-get-outta-trouble scenarios. And Grandma never bothered with lectures about love. With Beth's mouse-brown hair, nondescript features, and sit-in-the-corner personality, that subject never seemed necessary.

She stared at his ticket book and the pen he held in his work-worn hands. Then she looked up into his Caribbean-blue eyes. Big mistake. Everything else disappeared—bees, orchard, blossoms. Even fear took flight.

Love at first sight? Or even second sight? That was a fallacy, right? Relationships required more than physical attraction.

He quirked an eyebrow, and a gorgeous smile lit his eyes.

She snapped her gaze back to the ticket book. Should she? Well, why not? She hadn't done anything spontaneous since … when? … third grade? She snatched his pen and wrote on his palm.

Her face blazed. That was stupid. But too late to take it back now. She returned the pen, not daring to look up. One glance into those tranquil blue depths would undo her for sure.

Her sensible inner voice whispered above the babbling bees. *Start the car. Buckle up. Pull out slowly. Breathe.*

As she drove onto the road, her eyes strayed for one last look in her side mirror. The officer waved. With her phone number scrawled across his hand.

What was she going to tell her grandparents when she showed up late for dinner? Not a word. If she mentioned getting pulled over, Grandma would wheedle the whole story out of her. And Grandpa would pitch a fit.

As she mentally scrolled through acceptable excuses for not coming over for spaghetti after all, another thought swept into her head. The scenario unfolded like a scene from *America's Most Wanted*.

"The perpetrator goes to great lengths to impersonate an officer of the law," the monotone announcer's voice droned. "He has a uniform, a badge, and—"

Did he have a badge? She should've looked. At least gotten his name.

"He stole a police car and removed its tracking system. This criminal stops women on back roads and charms them into giving him their phone numbers. Once armed with this information, he arranges secluded meetings with his victims. This man has left a string of dead bodies from New York to California. He is considered armed and extremely dangerous, and was last seen in the vicinity of—"

Snap out of it. Beth shuddered, switched on the radio, and let slow jazz fill her car. Relaxing, she considered the depth of the officer's eyes, the way her fears melted at his smile. Whatever his name was, this guy was no criminal.

But she'd watch the local news tonight anyway.

Beth pulled into a parking lot and called Grandma on her cell phone. She didn't have to fake an excuse—a headache lurked at the base of her skull.

"No, it's nothing major. I just think I should go straight home tonight."

As her grandmother asked the first anticipated question, Beth sent her an eye roll. "Yes, I'll go right to bed. I'm sure I'll be fine in the morning. Talk to you tomorrow. Love you. Bye."

The tension in her shoulders dissolved as she rounded the corner onto her street. Her little blue house with white trim always made her smile. Inside she would find comfort in leftover Chinese take-out, a hot bath, and the last three chapters of a murder mystery.

As she stepped up to her front porch, a flash of yellow caught her eye. A bundle of roses lay on her doorstep. Two admirers in one day? Unheard of. She glanced around. Most of her neighbors had lived there forever. And someone always kept an eye out their window. The delivery wouldn't have gone unnoticed.

Beth scooped up the flowers, jogged across the street, and knocked.

Erma's door sprang open. Her crooked finger stroked the edge of a red petal. "You need to get these in water right away, dear. They're Judy Garlands—you can tell by the scent."

"Would you like one?" Beth eased a rose from the bundle.

"Won't your sweetheart mind?"

How much should she admit to the self-appointed neighborhood watch patrol? "Oh, they're probably from Grandpa."

Erma's lips quivered into a grin. "Well, the man who delivered those flowers was not the Grandpa I've met. He was tall and handsome. In his late twenties. And had a body like …" Crimson blossomed in her wrinkled cheeks. "Well, when he pulled up in his jeep and got out in that police uniform carrying a bouquet, he looked like the main attraction for a bachelorette party."

Beth cringed. That certainly fit the description of her— uh, of the officer who'd pulled her over. But surely he wouldn't have done this.

"I figured he must have the wrong house, because you're not seeing anyone. Are you, dear?"

Beth's world spun like a merry-go-round she couldn't get off of. "You're right. I need to get these in water."

Back in her house, she peeled the cellophane off the bouquet. A little card tumbled to the counter. Her name, written in neat capital letters, graced the front of the envelope. She pulled out the fix-it ticket and compared the handwriting. It matched.

He didn't seem like the stalker type. But he did know her name … and where she lived.

Beth trimmed the ends off the stems and arranged the roses in a vase. Each snip bolstered her courage to read the note.

Task done, she slipped her finger under the flap and popped the envelope open. With trembling hands, she removed the card. Three capital letters were printed there: JOS. Apparently he didn't want to tell her his real name. An Internet search of the tri-county area would come up with hundreds of possible suspects with those initials.

She tossed the card back on the counter. "If you want me to know your name, you'll just have to call me."

As if in answer, her cell phone trilled. Beth took three swipes on the screen to connect the call. And another two deep breaths to find her voice. "Hello?"

"Hi, Beth. It's Joss."

"What kind of a name is that?" She slapped her hand over her mouth and dropped onto the couch, mortified at the rude words that had slipped past her lips.

He laughed. "My brother couldn't say Joshua when I was born."

"And the nickname stuck. I get that. I have a brother too."

"I've been thinking … I could fix that taillight before you go to work tomorrow morning."

"Really?" She hugged a throw pillow to her chest to keep her heart from escaping. "I leave at seven."

"Good. Then I'll see you at six thirty, JB."

Had she heard him right? "Wait. How did you know—"

Click.

Beth's finger hovered over the redial button, itching to press it. Only her brother called her JB—his teasing nickname for *Just Beth*. And three years ago, Tim had tried to set her up on a date. With a cop. Named Joshua. She'd said no.

The truth pulled a smile across her face. Her admirer wasn't a random stranger after all.

Lead him on a full pursuit, urged the voice in her head. This time she'd listen.

Life Application

The most beautiful love story in the world is how God, the Creator of the universe, seeks a relationship with us, His most treasured creation. God calls people to Himself in myriad ways. Sometimes through the words of a friend. Or a favorite Scripture verse. The beauty of a sunset. A hummingbird cruising a backyard garden. If we listen with our hearts, we can hear His still small voice inviting us into an ever-deepening relationship. And our love for Him comes as a result of His loving us first (1 John 4:19).

How did God introduce Himself to you? How is He wooing and pursuing you into His presence today?

About the Author

Julie Williams works as a freelance editor and typographer for Inspire Press. She writes historical fiction, dabbles in allegory, and is trying her hand at fairy tale. On her days off, she enjoys being immersed in God's creation, as long as there's a hot shower and a soft bed awaiting her at the end of the day. Learn more about Julie at juliewilliams.us.

19

An American Valentine's Day

by Roxanne Anderson

Arjun pulled out his leftover eggplant curry from the mini-fridge and heated it up in the spattered microwave in the tiny office break room. As he sat down at the wobbly card table and dug into his wife's delicious food, he tuned in to the conversation of the other three occupants of the room. Josh and David were having an animated discussion with Susan. It took Arjun a while to catch up to the topic. His English was flawless, but the way Americans pronounced their words and used so much slang sometimes made it difficult to follow.

"I was in the doghouse for a month after I dropped the ball last year," Josh admitted as he poured coffee into a foam cup.

"What'd you give her?" Susan opened her Greek yogurt and stirred it with a plastic spoon. Arjun took a bite of his own spicy meal and felt sorry for Susan having to eat such bland food.

"A felt rose I picked up at 7-Eleven after work." Josh kicked the side of the frayed loveseat where Susan was sitting.

She snorted. "Well, yeah. I'd have kicked my boyfriend to the curb for a stupid stunt like that too."

David laughed as he spread mayonnaise on his sandwich. "Hey, I've made some pretty dumb mistakes myself. A couple of years ago I thought I was being real smart to take my wife someplace nice for dinner. Totally escaped me that Valentine's Day is one of the most booked-up nights of the year and I didn't think to make reservations. We hired a sitter, Melissa got all dressed up, and when we arrived at this fancy place she'd been dying to go to, we were told it would be a three-hour wait. We ended up at a pizza parlor. Not my finest Valentine's Day moment."

Arjun stopped eating. "What is Valentine's Day?"

Susan chuckled. "It's the most important American holiday … if you want to keep your significant other happy."

They all filled him in on the best traditional gifts: red roses, chocolate candy in heart-shaped boxes, jewelry, stuffed animals, romantic surprises, and fancy dinners in expensive restaurants.

By the time Arjun returned to his desk, his head was spinning. He'd been trying hard to fit into American culture. Nisha kept up with the native festivals, so she undoubtedly knew all about this one. If his coworkers were right, he should definitely buy her a gift on this auspicious day for marriage blessings.

Arjun and his wife never ate out. He didn't have time to order a properly made piece of jewelry and couldn't afford one anyway. But Nisha did like sweets.

When Arjun left the office, he bypassed the Hong Kong market where he usually bought their vegetables and went to an American grocery store to look for candy.

In one crowded aisle, he encountered a sea of red. He must be in the right place. But now what? He had never seen so many hearts in all his life. Harried-looking shoppers grabbed candy, stuffed animals, and greeting cards off the shelves as if their lives depended on the purchases.

After careful consideration, Arjun selected a medium-sized heart-shaped velvet box—the same color as the sari Nisha wore on their wedding day. As he stood impatiently in the long line at the check-out counter, then inched his way home in five o'clock traffic, he imagined the look on his wife's face when he presented his gift to her.

When he finally pulled into a parking space behind their apartment complex, he raced up the three flights of stairs to their home. Opening the door, he saw Nisha in the kitchen, standing in front of the stove, enveloped in pungent steam. Before he could say anything, she asked in Hindi, "Did you bring the tomatoes? I'm ready to put them in the curry."

Arjun stopped cold. The tomatoes! Valentine's Day had driven them from his mind completely.

Nisha turned around impatiently. He winced, and she read the answer in his face. "Really? I ask you to bring just one thing and you forget even that?"

Arjun took a tentative step toward her and held out the red box, at a loss for what to say. Ignoring him, she went back to cooking, stirring the food vigorously.

He put the box on counter. His wife pointed at it with her spoon. "What is that?"

He shrugged. "It's for Valentine's Day. The American love festival."

Nisha put down the spoon and wiped her hands on a towel. "Jennifer was telling me about that in the laundry room this morning. But she didn't call it a love festival."

"What is it, then?"

"She said it has something to do with a God of love and His Son." She picked up a folded piece of paper off the counter.

Arjun took the flyer and peered at the cover. "God is love" was printed in black letters over a red heart. He opened the pamphlet. But before he could start reading, his wife drew in a quick breath. He looked up. The delighted expression on her face as she peeked inside the candy box was everything he had imagined it would be.

Nisha traced the velvet heart with her fingertips. "Never mind the tomatoes," she whispered.

After dinner, they took the box of chocolates and the little booklet to the living room, where they read it together.

"What are these Four Spiritual Laws?" Arjun questioned. "Do the spirits in America have different laws from ours?" He glanced at the picture of Shiva, the main Hindu god, on the wall. He and Nisha did their best to stay on good terms with all the gods.

"It says here that this God loves us and has a wonderful plan for our lives," Nisha commented.

They read on, often stopping to discuss unfamiliar terms and concepts. When they'd finished, Arjun shook his head. "I'm still confused as to what these spiritual laws have to do with Valentine's Day."

Nisha nibbled a chocolate. "Jennifer said that God's love for us is stronger and more faithful than any human love. She also said that every person has a God-shaped hole inside of them that can only be filled with His love, even though people often try to fill the hole with things or with human love."

Could that be why his coworkers had been so focused on buying things for this holiday?

"Jennifer says it is important to remember God's love the most on Valentine's Day."

Arjun frowned. "But which god? There are so many."

"This booklet says his name is Jesus." Nisha tapped the paper with her fingernail, clinking the bangles on her wrist. "He is the only god I have heard about who loved people enough to die for their sins."

Arjun wanted to find out more about this god and His love. But at the moment, he had something else on his mind. He set the flyer on the coffee table and gazed at his beautiful wife. "So, if you get God's love for Valentine's Day ... does that mean you don't need chocolates?"

Nisha tipped her head playfully. "Oh, I will always need the love of my husband too. And if in America husbands bring chocolates to their wives once a year on Valentine's Day, that should happen in our home as well."

Warmth filled Arjun's heart. "Well, then …" He leaned close to his wife. "Happy American Valentine's Day."

Life Application

Celebrating Valentine's Day has become highly commercial. But shouldn't a holiday dedicated to love turn our thoughts and attention to the God who loves us far more than anyone else ever could? And what better way to celebrate His love than by sharing it with others?

Every day, there are people all around us who need to hear the good news—in the grocery store, at the mall, at work and the park, in our schools. John 15:12 says, "This is My commandment, that you love one another as I have loved you" (NKJV).

God loved us enough to send His Son, Jesus, to die for our sins. That's the greatest love story of all time.

About the Author

Roxanne Anderson spent several years doing full-time missionary work in India, Nepal, Hong Kong, and West Africa. She currently lives in Dallas, Texas. Her life is passionately defined by parenting three teenagers, her work as a midwife, supporting missions, and writing. She blogs about all these things at roxanneswildworld.blogspot.com.

20

Rose in Bloom

by Jennifer Sienes

ho needs a husband and babies when I have all this?" Kennedy Rose swept her hand Vanna-White-style to encompass her florist shop. Amaryllis, carnations, delphinium, oriental lilies, tulips, daffodils, and, of course, roses. Riotous spring color on this frosty February 13th.

Her proclamation was met with an unladylike snort. "You keep telling yourself that." Maggie waggled a sprig of baby's breath at her. "It'll be small comfort in your old age." She rubbed her T-shirt-clad baby bump, which was growing larger by the day.

As Kennedy watched her best friend caress what would soon be child number two, a pang of envy squeezed her heart. Or maybe it was the sriracha sauce she'd doused her pot stickers with at lunch. Whatever. She focused on the glittery red hearts she'd stuck in the storefront the week before. "When the right man comes along—"

"You'll be so buried in blooms, you won't recognize him." Maggie retrieved her purse from behind the counter. "Thanks for lunch. I hate to eat and run, but I want to get home before Cody wakes up from his nap."

"No problem." She had to admit, the scent of Cody's petal-soft neck could rival that of an American Beauty rose.

"And when Jason comes in tomorrow for my Valentine's bouquet, remind him I like *pink* roses. Or red. Not yellow." She shook her head. "Where he got the idea that yellow means romance, I don't know."

"Be thankful you have a husband who cares enough to buy you flowers at all." Kennedy winced. She'd become her mother. When did *that* happen?

Maggie stopped, one hand on the door, eyebrow cocked. "You know what your problem is?"

"My biological clock?"

"You're too picky."

"I have standards, my friend. And they aren't even that high. All I ask is that the man I marry be faithful, kind, and romantic." She raised a finger. "Oh, and employed."

"You're looking for a Boy Scout, not a husband."

"I'm not *looking* at all." Waiting, but not looking.

"That's another one of your problems. You think the perfect man is going to just appear out of nowhere. But as long as you're holed up in this shop, the only men you'll meet are the ones who are already attached." She pulled the door open and nearly collided with a man who was entering.

He side-stepped and held the door open. "After you."

Kennedy squelched a bark of laughter at Maggie's exaggerated swoon through the storefront window behind his back.

"Have I done something amusing?" The deep voice drew her attention away from her friend's antics.

A pair of hydrangea-blue eyes sucked the air from her lungs.

"Uh, not at all." Face warm, Kennedy snatched up the flowers she'd been arranging. An amateur move, she realized when a hot stab of pain shot through her hand. Disengaging the thorn, she pressed her thumb against her green canvass apron to soak up the drop of blood. "What can I do for you?"

He motioned to her hand. "You okay?"

"Oh, just peachy." The warmth in her cheeks rose a degree or two. "I assume you're here for flowers."

He nodded. "You assume correctly. I'd like something for a very special lady."

Of course. "Roses *are* the flower of choice this time of year."

He squinted. "Too cliché, don't you think?"

"That's entirely up to you."

He perused the shop. "Nice place you've got." He wrinkled his nose. "But doesn't the heavy aroma of flowers get to you after a while?"

Kennedy inhaled. "Nope. I love it. It's eternally spring in here."

He took her business card from the holder by the register. "Kennedy Rose?"

"Actually, it's Kennedy Rose Marin. But for business reasons, I opted to drop my last name."

"I'm Trent Carter." He stuck out his hand. His warm fingers enveloped hers.

A zing of heat shot through her. She tugged her hand free.

"Have you worked here long?"

"I own the shop."

"Then you must be an expert at picking out just the right bouquet."

He had her there. "Tell me something about the recipient and I'll see what I can do."

"She's adventurous. Loves nature, babies, and romance."

"Well, who doesn't?" They shared a grin.

Was this to be her destiny? Helping attractive men pick out just the right flowers to woo their girlfriends and wives? "Is she a traditionalist or a trendsetter?"

He tilted his head. "She's a classy lady. But spontaneous enough to sport a hot-pink streak in her hair."

Kennedy did a mental eye-roll. "I put together some bouquets this morning that might be perfect for her." She slipped from behind the counter and walked to one of the glass-fronted refrigerator units. "If pink's her color, there are a few here that might be to her liking." She motioned to the shelves of bouquets. "What do you think?"

"I think you have beautiful green eyes."

Was he was flirting with her while picking out flowers for a girlfriend? Of all the nerve! "I *meant* the flowers."

He pointed to a collection of gladiolas, amaryllis, and delphinium. "I'll take those."

"Fine." She grabbed the vase and marched back to the counter. The sooner she got this guy out of her shop, the better. "Would you like a card to go with them?" Her voice was frostier than the vase, but she didn't care. He deserved the cold shoulder.

"Have I offended you in some way?"

"Not at all." She sniffed. "I'll just ring these up for you." Her fingers fumbled at the register. Lips tight, she slid his purchase toward him. "I hope your girlfriend enjoys them." The words were forced through gritted teeth.

His baby blues crinkled with confusion. "These aren't for my girlfriend."

Wife, then. Even worse! "It's really no business of mine who they're for."

After paying for the flowers, he pulled out a small card and set it on the counter. "I'd love it if you'd call me sometime."

Was he kidding?

Before the door closed behind him, Kennedy tossed the card into the trash without even reading it.

The Rose Garden was hopping all day long on February 14th. Husbands and boyfriends who'd waited until the last minute converged on the shop like a swarm of locusts and left nothing behind but a few sorry-looking bouquets. Valentine's Day was always good for business, but that didn't soothe Kennedy's ego much.

What's wrong with me? One minute she denied the desire for a husband, and the next she was moping about not having one.

Head buried in the refrigerator, Kennedy was gathering up fallen leaves and a collection of wilted stems when the tinkle of the bell over the door caught her attention. "I'm afraid I don't have much left," she said without turning.

"Oh, you might be surprised."

Spinning toward the melodic voice, her nose nearly collided with the refrigerator door. A puff of cold air escaped from her mouth.

An elderly woman stood in the doorway of the shop. Her hair was pure white with one bold streak of hot pink. This couldn't be Trenton Carter's amour, could it?

"I'm Amelia Carter." She took three sure steps, shoulders back and a mischievous grin on her lips. "Might you be Kennedy Rose?"

She nodded.

"I'm Trent's grandmother." Her dainty hand gave Kennedy's a firm squeeze. "The flowers were lovely."

"So he's not—" Kennedy snapped her lips shut. She wouldn't look good with her size sevens crammed inside her mouth.

"Not what?" The twinkle in her eye bespoke amusement.

She gulped. "Attached?"

"I suppose that would depend on you, dear."

Kennedy bit her cheek in an effort to hold in the silly grin that was trying its best to break free.

"My grandson would be appalled if he knew I was here. But you were all he talked about at dinner last night. You and your charming store." She held up a crooked finger. "I think he might be smitten."

Air would be good right now. And some sort of comprehensible reply.

"I hope to see you again, Miss Kennedy Rose." Amelia left with a wave and a smile.

The sweet woman wasn't quite out of sight before Kennedy dove toward the trash can.

Life Application

In this world of independence and impatience, we are often on the fast track to disappointment. We want what we want *now* and don't trust God, in His infinite wisdom, to come through for us. Rather than wait on His timing, we step around Him. But if we delight in Him first, He will bestow on us the desires of our hearts.

What is it that you have been waiting for? Have you given it to the Lord and trusted that He has a perfect plan for you? Or are you striving to make it happen in your strength and timing?

About the Author

Jennifer Sienes gave up teaching to write full time. She is a 2013 Genesis semifinalist and a 2014 Genesis winner for the contemporary fiction category. She has three short stories published in *Inspire Faith* and another in *Chicken Soup for the Soul: Recovering from Traumatic Brain Injury*.

21

Bring Him Home

by Susan May Warren

Four minutes into the third quarter, John's father decided to die. Not soon enough for John to ditch the game at halftime and catch a plane for northern Minnesota. But while he was still on the field, lining up to rush the quarterback.

John missed the tackle and landed hard on the tuff. The taste of frustration locked in his teeth as a perfect pass drifted into the hands of the wideout standing just inside the end zone.

He should have simply stayed there, not gotten up to hear the news. No more second chances for the prodigal who'd left home without looking back.

John pulled into the resort parking lot, steadying the Moose club's floral arrangement next to him on the truck's passenger seat, thankful to have finally pried himself out of the suffocating congregation from the memorial service. It was quite possible his father knew everyone in northern Minnesota, and most of them had driven from the far reaches of the state to say their last good-byes.

All, of course, but Ingrid. John had looked for her, more times than he wanted to admit, felt her absence as a hollowness in his chest. He'd thought, of all times Ingrid might forgive him, it would be today.

Grabbing the floral arrangement, he climbed out into the piney fragrance of the north woods retreat. "I'll be back to get the box of casserole dishes in a minute," he said to his mother as she struggled to climb out of the truck's backseat. He should have taken his father's old Buick to the cemetery, but he couldn't find the keys in the mess of the resort office.

John set the arrangement on the kitchen countertop and paused, the view of the lake just beyond his parents' sliding glass doors calling to him. Pristine blue water lapped against the dilapidated dock, shaggy evergreens waved in the wind, and cirrus dragged across the sky as if the sun might be a reluctant traveler on this mournful day.

"He never fixed the dock," John said.

"He left that for the new owner." Mom dropped her purse on the bench by the door.

John tried to shrug off her words. After two generations, the legacy of the Evergreen family resort would pass to different—unfamiliar—hands.

And whose fault was that?

He returned to the car, retrieved the box of casseroles, and set it on the counter. "How long before the resort changes hands?"

His mother's lined face, which had aged a decade in the last year, put a knife in his chest. Dad owed them all an explanation for his secrecy. Who hears a diagnosis of cancer and doesn't fight it? Or doesn't at least call his only son to come home and take the helm?

But a man didn't survive in the north woods of Minnesota without a Norwegian stubborn streak. Clearly John had inherited that from his old man.

Still, his father could have done something to prepare them, maybe even allowed John to pick up the pieces. Then he might have had a reason to go after Ingrid and beg her forgiveness. Convince her that yes, he really did believe in her dreams.

"The new owner will take over soon," his mother replied. "I made arrangements to go live with my sister in Minneapolis. Maybe I can finally watch one of your games."

"Please don't," he said, but it emerged in a mumble, the truth brittle and raw-edged. He'd made his choices, and they'd backfired. He hadn't made the NFL, and Arena ball only bandaged the wounds, didn't heal them.

"Nathan Decker is coming over later with some paperwork." His mother loaded the casseroles into the freezer, rearranging to find space. They could eat for a year off the generosity of their small town. "He's making a name for himself in the real estate business now that his mother is over her cancer." Not a flicker of resentment that maybe, just maybe, God might have spared her husband too.

"I can't believe Nate stuck around. He had a cross-country scholarship."

"Some people simply belong in Deep Haven, honey."

Like him?

Mom patted his arm. "By the way, the sink is leaking. Could you take a look?"

He climbed under the counter and found soggy wood from where the pipe leaked. "How long has it been like this?"

"Oh, a year or so."

Of course. Judging by the state of the entire resort, his father had abandoned any repairs long ago. As if he'd already resigned them to the next owner. Instead of asking his son for help. Stubborn man.

"I need tools."

"Look in the garage."

John headed outside, past the potholed basketball court. A shadowy memory crossed his mind. The old man seated on the steps, under the glow of the porch light thick with flirting moths. *Soft hands, Son!* Dad's voice lingered in the breeze, correcting, encouraging.

John flicked on the light in the garage, then paused for a moment, inhaling the redolence of grease soaked into the dirt floor, a century of oil and gasoline embedded in the walls. The ancient Raider twin-track snow machine sat dormant, a relic of forgotten days.

He headed toward the tools scattered along the far work-bench, then squeezed around a long, tarped object propped on saw horses.

He bumped it and it tipped. He caught it, his grip curving around the edges.

No. It couldn't be. He paused for a moment, his heart wedged in his throat, before he flung off the tarp.

The canoe. The hand-hewn wooden art project that had consumed his junior-year summer. John ran his hand over the keel, expecting to rut against the gash where he'd ran it onto the rocks that last summer at home. Instead, he felt smooth, fresh wood.

"He spent all last spring on it. His last project." His mother stood in the doorway, her eyes glistening. "You should take it out."

Maybe … one last time. Just to say good-bye. He hoisted it up by the portage pads and carried it to the lake. A summer wind skimmed the surface as he flipped it and lowered it into the lake. The paddles were lodged in the gun whales and he climbed in the back and retrieved them.

The canoe slipped like a prayer onto the pristine waters.

Silence, the peace of water lapping against the edges, a collection of memories in the wind. Fishing off the stern, jumping from the bow. Laughter as his father swamped the canoe.

Then he saw it—his name, etched in the crossbar next to his father's. He reached out and ran his fingers into the grooves. His eyes burned. "Why didn't you tell me, Dad?"

A loon answered mourning across the blue.

In the quiet, John's own voice echoed back.

"I don't want your land, or your resort. I want my own life."

He'd gotten what he asked for.

But not what he truly wanted.

The thought gathered beneath him, sluicing heat through his chest, like he might be lining up for a play. This life—the insignificant, quiet life of working the family legacy—*was* his life. Or at least he wanted it to be.

Maybe his father had called him home after all.

John turned toward the dock and paddled into the sun, tasting the evergreen, the loam of the land, rich, decadent.

He spotted a woman standing on the dock, wearing a white sundress, the sun bronzing her silky blonde hair.

Ingrid raised her hand and smiled, forgiveness in her beautiful blue eyes.

He pulled up to the dock, his heart so large in his chest it burned. "What are you doing here?"

"Your mother called. Said you'd just inherited a resort and you might be in need of a wife." She lifted a shoulder, her smile sweet and tentative.

"I do," John said, his voice breaking. The canoe slid up to the dock and he reached out for her.

She took his hand, pulled him to shore. Wrapped her arms around his neck, lifting her face to his. Her kiss was everything he remembered.

All that he needed.

And there, under the late-afternoon sun, he finally heard the voice of his father, cheering.

Life Application

Have you ever found yourself so far away from your home, your dreams, your plans, your hopes, that it feels like there's no way back? Have you stood in that moment and felt the loneliness of your life shake you? I remember the day when I realized I was walking a path that had no future, a path of self-destruction.

Stubborn in my mistakes, I loathed to acknowledge my lostness. But I longed for a different life. One that would lead me to my happy ending.

My error was in believing that I had to create it.

In that darkness, a sliver of light broke through as I recalled Jeremiah 29:11–12. *"I know the plans I have for you,"* *declares the LORD.*

Plans? For me?

"Plans to prosper you and not to harm you, plans to give you hope and a future."

I wanted that. But how?

"Then you will call on me and come and pray to me, and I will listen to you."

God would listen to me? After everything I'd done, I didn't even want to listen to myself.

And yet … there He was, whispering hope, peace, joy, and purpose into my life.

What if God has made this easy? What if He's gone before you to set up your happy ending, and all you have to do is walk into it? Accept it? Embrace it? Surrender to it?

Today is your day to stop wandering … and come home.

About the Author

Susan May Warren is the Christy, RITA, and Carol award-winning author of more than forty-five novels with Tyndale, Barbour, Steeple Hill, and Summerside Press. A prolific novelist with more than one million books sold, Susan has written contemporary and historical romances, romantic suspense, thrillers, rom-com, and Christmas novellas. She loves to help people launch their writing careers and is the founder of MyBookTherapy.com and LearnHowtoWriteaNovel.com, a website that helps authors get published and stay published. She's also the author of the popular writing method The Story Equation. Find excerpts and reviews of her novels at susanmaywarren.com.

$\mathcal{J}$s there anything better in all the world than love? Love is a universal language that transcends geography, culture, even religious beliefs.

Mahatma Gandhi said, "Where there is love there is life." Saint Augustine said, "Love is the beauty of the soul." Charles Dickens said, "A loving heart is the truest wisdom." Oliver Wendell Holmes said, "Love is the master key which opens the gates of happiness."[1]

So why not celebrate Valentine's Day all through the year? Every day we can show love in tangible ways … to family members, friends, mere acquaintances, even strangers. We can do this through a kind word, a thoughtful gesture, a personal gift, an offer to pray, or just a smile.

When our lives are topsy-turvy, overly busy, or filled with pain, it can be difficult to feel loving toward others. We yearn to receive love more than to give it. How can we share with someone else if our own supply is empty?

There is one never-ending, eternal source of unfathomable love, a wellspring from which we can draw when our souls feel bone dry. The Bible says, "There is no greater love than to lay down one's life for one's friends" (John 15:13 NLT).

---

[1] Quotes from http://en.proverbia.net/.

That's what Jesus did for each of us. He willingly gave up His life to pay the penalty for our sins so that we could be called friends of God. He did this out of a heart of pure, passionate, perfect love.

If you haven't experienced God's love yet, or if it's been a while since you felt it permeate your soul, talk to Him. And read His "love letter" to you, the Bible. Especially the Gospels (the first four books of the New Testament). No matter where you are or what you've done, your heavenly Father is eager to fill your heart with His abundant, free gift of love.

If you've been impacted or blessed by any of the stories in this book, may I encourage you to share that experience with others? Visit our website, FictionDevo.com, and find the forum on "21 Days of Love." Read what others have said about the stories in this book, and post something yourself about what a particular story meant to you.

If you prefer a more casual setting, visit facebook.com/FictionDevo to read and write posts about all of the books in the Fiction Lover's Devotional series.

More Books in This Series

Look for more books in this series
from BroadStreet Publishing

21 Days of Grace:
Stories that Celebrate God's Unconditional Love

21 Days of Christmas:
Stories that Celebrate God's Greatest Gift

21 Days of Joy:
Stories that Celebrate Motherhood

Alphabetical List of Contributing Authors